SIR BERNEY BROGRAVE
A Very Anxious Man

The real story behind the legend of Norfolk's most notorious ghost

Cheryl Nicol

Copyright © 2015 Cheryl Nicol
All rights reserved.
ISBN-10: 1518771971
ISBN-13: 978-1518771972

TABLE OF CONTENTS

Introduction i
Chapter 1 1
  The Legend 1
Chapter 2 9
  The Early Years 9
  Marriage, Family, and the Sweet Smell of… Effluvia?? 17
Chapter 3 27
  A Target of Criticism and Cannonballs 27
  A Slightly Exaggerated Report 31
Chapter 4 43
  Sir Berney's Battle with the Sea 43
  Letters to Marquis Townshend 51
Chapter 5 59
  Two Eventful Years; 1790-92 59
Chapter 6 65
  The Beginning of the End for Berney 65
Chapter 7 71
  A Family in Decline 71
  Berney's Siblings 73
    The Lawyer; Thomas Brograve 73
    The Naval Officer; Captain William Brograve 77
    The Plantation Owner's Wife; Elizabeth Brograve 87
    The Prim Spinster; Anne Brograve 89
Chapter 8 93
  The Survivors 93
    Sir George Berney Brograve, 2nd Baronet 93
    Lady Brograve's 'Criminal Conversation' 97
    Captain Roger Brograve - On a Hiding to Nothing 108
    Anne Rye, nee Brograve - The Dilemma of the 'Half-blood' 112
Chapter 9 117
  A Diminished Legacy 117
  The Last Gasp 126
Chapter 10 135
  Waxham Hall 135
  Worstead House 141
Chapter 11 147
  Extinction of a Dynasty 147
  The Final Curtain 151

Introduction

Just below the windswept veneer of East Anglia runs a rich seam of ghost stories, tales of shipwrecks, smuggling and villages lost to the sea. Contributing to its history is the 250 year-old legend of Sir Berney Brograve of Waxham Hall, ingrained in folklore for generations as an infamous despot in league with the devil.

His larger-than-life persona reinforced the negative perception in the villager's minds. But was he really as bad as his reputation would have us believe, or was he merely misunderstood? The short answer is - both.

Well-educated and well-married, his forebears had ridden a wave of privilege and prosperity for centuries. Grand houses. Armies of servants. They passed their name and accumulated wealth successively from father to son. But Berney's inheritance came with unwelcome extras.

His sixteenth century manor house Waxham Hall sits precariously on the crumbling edge of a beautiful, wild and desolate Norfolk landscape. Once known as Devil's Country, Waxham has been described even by its own inhabitants as a rum old place at the best of times. They wouldn't recommend being out alone on a dark night in case the ghost of old Sir Berney happened to be about.

The reconstruction of his life reveals many anxieties. He was a staunch patriot intolerant of disloyalty and injustice, prepared to fight for king and country. He didn't recognise his worst enemy, however. He enjoyed the acquaintance of several high-profile individuals but his inability to contain his frustrations and communicate with any tact or diplomacy became his downfall.

He was a man blighted by misfortune. His land flooded year after year. Death decimated his family. The threat of French invasion kept him on the edge of his seat and the activities of smugglers kept him awake at night. The ingredient common to these menaces - the sea - insidiously undermined his sanity with each destructive inundation of his land. This is the real story behind the legend.

Chapter 1
The Legend

Sir Berney Brograve sold his soul to the devil, so said the villagers of East Norfolk. They despised and feared him in equal measure; he had terrorised them for years. When he died in March 1797 there was great rejoicing; they were free from his tyranny at last. But their joy was short-lived. Soon taverns and alehouses were abuzz with wild-eyed talk. Even strong burly men were frightened out of their wits on encountering Sir Berney's ghost roaming his wild and desolate domain in the dark of night. Cape flying, his horse snorted fire from its nostrils, the devil by his side.

Great fodder for fertile imaginations, his notoriously volatile temperament is the subject of many tall tales, cementing his place in history. Far from being the wicked and evil character portrayed in legend, the squire of Waxham nevertheless attracted plenty of criticism for his flint-heartedness and miserly ways. Certainly his communication skills left a lot to be desired. From these seeds grew tall stories, posthumously magnified and embellished by local story-tellers.

There is much more to the story, however. Behind the scenes, Berney (pronounced 'Barney') was an extremely anxious man.

No ghost story mentions his ongoing and at times comical battles with smugglers. Nor is there any mention of the toll taken on his young family after the North Sea inundated his estate year after year, leaving behind a hazardous environment which led to disease and death.

Many villagers perished. Also dead in its wake were his crops, most of his seventeen children and both his wives. No one would help him mend the sea breaches to slow the savage erosion of his slice of crumbling Norfolk coastline. He had more bad luck than most, but there was no sympathy for this short-tempered man.

The raging sea wasn't the only problem. He was afraid Napoleon's army would take a shortcut through his vulnerable seafront property to invade England.

Come what may, Berney was determined not to abandon his troublesome coastal estate at Waxham in favour of his newer house high and dry at Worstead. Worstead House was a gentleman's mansion with pleasure gardens, whereas Waxham was a highly productive farm when it wasn't underwater or fetidly drying out. It was part of his inheritance from his father and he wouldn't give in. Not to the sea. Not to anyone. It was a stance he would live to regret; ultimately there was a price to pay for his single-minded determination.

Embroidered a little more with each retelling, the tales passed down by the East Norfolk villagers ensured the immortality of the lord of Waxham, Horsey, Sea Palling and Worstead. Berney was seen as a tyrannical oppressor by his poor tenants who scraped a living as he reaped their rents and tithes. A stubborn and irascible character, his strong sense of loyalty and justice were not seen as positive attributes by those on the receiving end.

Berney's exaggerated reputation for audacity and cunning inspired the tale that he had once outwitted the devil after recklessly boasting he would stake his soul in a mowing match. By secretly planting the devil's acre with iron rods he easily won the bet. The story goes that the devil had to stop several times to sharpen his scythe, and on seeing Berney finish first he cried out: 'I say Barney Bor, them bunks do cut damned hard!' These words were repeated long afterwards by Worstead mowers when thistles blunted their scythes.

As recently as the 1920's Norfolk antiquary Walter Rye remarked that the legend of Sir Berney was still green in the memories of the older inhabitants of East Norfolk. 'Everybody out Stalham way knew that 'Owd Sir Barney' rode on certain nights in the year along the 'Carnser' [causeway] from Waxham Hall to Worstead. If no one could be produced who had really seen the apparition, why, there was any number who had 'heard tell' of it.' At the same time W.H Cooke, historian and avid collector of Norfolk folklore, related the story of the Haunted Chamber in the attic at Waxham Hall. One of the Brograves had committed suicide by cutting his own throat and bloodstains are said to reappear on the walls at certain times of the year.

The hoary antiquity and later neglect of the old hall lent itself perfectly to another story; the haunting by a 'somewhat numerous ghostly train' of spirits of six Brograves of earlier generations separated by several centuries. These characters date from Sir Ralph at the Crusades, with Sir Edmund in the Barons' War, Sir John at Agincourt, Sir Francis in the Wars of the Roses, Sir Thomas during the Civil War and Sir Charles at Ramillies. All were supposed to have died violently in battle. In reality Sir Thomas died peacefully in 1670, nearly twenty years after the English Civil War had ended, and there appears to be no such person named Sir Charles Brograve alive at the time of the Battle of Ramillies in 1706.

Not allowing facts to get in the way of a good story, Berney reputedly invited them all to dinner one New Year's Eve, solemnly drinking a toast to each one praising their valour, after which he roared a few old Norfolk ballads and finished off all their wine. Suddenly, at the stroke of midnight, the ghostly apparitions vanished. Berney later awoke, cold and irritable, presumably nursing an all-too-familiar hangover.

After another heavy drinking session he is said to have taken refuge in Brograve Mill while being chased by the devil. Terrified, he spent the night locked in the mill with the sound of hooves banging at the door. In the morning when he ventured out he found the mill door covered in hoof marks. If there is any basis in truth it may have been revenge perpetrated with some glee by disgruntled villagers. The fear of those on the receiving end of Berney's infamous verbal rants quickly turned to contempt, and the opportunity to get their own back once in a while was considered a small compensation.

The numerous stories about Berney suggest he tore up the rulebook, disregarding the niceties of gentlemanly negotiation. He reserved his best behaviour for his peers. However he had his limits. He was congenial as long as the conversation remained agreeable to him, but his self-control was sorely tested if they failed to see his point of view. Even without lubrication he could quickly turn from quietly convivial to loud and verbal. Dispute resolution sometimes became a physical matter between himself and the villagers, and his fist-fights and wagers were legendary.

One such spectacle is said to have occurred after a chimney sweep cleaned out the chimneys at Waxham Hall. Berney was so outraged at the price when the sweep demanded payment he offered to fight him for the money. If the sweep won he would be paid double; if he lost he would get no money and probably a black eye or two into the bargain. Berney claimed victory after giving up at round three. His battering of the wretched sweep had raised such a cloud of soot that he almost choked and had to resort to a week of hard drinking to remove the taste.

About a hundred years ago a local marshman summed up Berney's reputation in the delightfully quirky Norfolk style:

> "Owd Sir Barney Brograve he wur a werry bad owd man and he sold his soul to th' Devil and guv him a parchment bond. When he died he went and called on the Devil and saa to him – 'Here I be' . . . but the Devil saa 'I've been looking trew your acount and it fare to me, if I hev you in

here 'twon't be a sennight afore yew'll be top dog and I'll have to play second fiddle, so there's your writing back and now be off - and Sir Barney, he saa, where am I to go tew' and the owd Devil he forgot hisself and saa 'Go to hell' . . . and Sir Barney had no idea of wandering all about nowhere, so he tuk him at his word and he sat down and stayed. And they du say there's tew Devils there now."[1]

The passing of two centuries has provided many opportunities for creative storytellers to embellish the yarns, to the extent that the subject himself has all but lost his identity. Or worse still, that he was not a real person but merely an imaginary character. Berney is identified correctly by Jennifer Westwood and Jacqueline Simpson (*The Lore of the Land: a Guide to England's Legends*) who refer to previous errors and confusion by folklorists, one perpetuated by the misspelling of his name as Sir Barnabas Bromgrave, and the assumption by another that 'the name of Sir Barnabas Brograve is a fictitious one.'

John Canning (*50 Strange Stories of the Supernatural*), describes Berney as 'the epitome of the raffish bachelor Squire' and an adventurous horseman of immense strength who could drink any of his neighbours under the table. The latter was quite probably true, but Canning was mistaken in believing that Sir Berney never married: 'He died a bachelor, but dotted the countryside with his portrait'. He may well have fathered numerous illegitimate children but certainly he didn't die a bachelor. In fact he outlived both his wives to whom he was lawfully wed, as well as thirteen of his seventeen legitimate children.

Although often germinated from a grain of truth, good yarns have little to do with historical accuracy. Two and a half centuries of accumulated Norfolk earth, mud and superstition has obscured the real story of Sir Berney Brograve. To discover his true character it is necessary to dig a little more below the surface.

---

[1] Found in an unpublished collection of notes on Norfolk legends by antiquarian William Blyth Gerish, quoted in The Lore of the Land: a Guide to England's Legends, (2005) by Jennifer Westwood and Jacqueline Simpson

Chapter 2
The Early Years

When Berney was born in October 1726 his mother Julian (granddaughter of Sir Richard Berney of Parkhall, Redeham) was counting her blessings her baby still had a father. Recently in court on a murder charge, her husband Thomas Brograve had avoided doing time in a dank London prison - or worse – execution. Six months earlier he had killed a man in a duel. Berney's parents had been married less than a year when his father was indicted for the murder of Henry Branthwaite, Julian's first cousin. Branthwaite, an attorney of the Middle Temple, had taken offence to Thomas making 'several very severe reflections' on his character.

Unable to forgive this affront Branthwaite planned a showdown; the proverbial pistols at dawn. Except he had to wait until the afternoon; Thomas was not at home when he called on him. According to witness statements at the subsequent Old Bailey trial, it was noon when Branthwaite tracked Thomas down to his usual Sunday haunt, George's Coffee Bar in Devereaux Street.

Typically a male dominated domain, it was one of hundreds of coffeehouses which had sprung up all over London to cater to the popular new coffee-drinking culture. George's was a place where wits and scholars came to listen and be heard. Every important event that took place in Britain was discussed *ad infinitum* over a cup of good strong brew, and although Thomas didn't yet realise it, he would soon become the latest topic of conversation.

After experiencing a very severe winter the inhabitants of London welcomed the warm spring weather of that February day, and surrounded by exotic aromas and the hubbub of conversation, Thomas made himself conspicuous by keeping his cloak on while he warmed himself by the fire. Some of the other patrons would later recall this detail, the inference being that he could have been concealing weapons. In fact he was not long out of his sick-bed and still felt a lingering chill. When he heard Branthwaite enquire after him at the bar, he shouted "Here!" On the pretext of Branthwaite's need to discuss a certain matter of business, they left together in a coach he had waiting at the door.

They were noticed by another witness on their arrival at Hyde Park who later told the court he saw two gentlemen in scarlet cloaks coming towards him 'pretty fast'. Against a backdrop of shrubbery and without the usual attendants, they threw their cloaks, hats and wigs to the ground and went down on their knees, pointing pistols at each other. What happened next is described by the witness:

> 'Says the Prisoner, Fire. No (says the Deceas'd) do you fire first - You ought to do that, says the Prisoner. - Well then, says the Deceas'd, let us fire both at once, and so they did, and both mist, then they drew their Swords. The Deceas'd ran toward the Prisoner, who parry'd off his

> Sword, and pusht at him. They closed, struggled together, the Deceas'd fell backward, and the Prisoner upon him; the Prisoner then took away the Deceas'd's Sword, and they both got up, but the Deceas'd stagger'd, and fell down again.'

Thomas was shocked at Branthwaite lying lifeless before him. The witness heard him say: 'Speak, who was in the Fault? Will ye forgive me? - Pray forgive me.' The court heard that Thomas's sword was bloody and crooked. He wiped it on the grass, straightened it then waved his hat for a coach at Hyde-Park Corner. A coach came; he put on his cloak, wig and hat, and asked the witness to take care of Branthwaite, promising to send a surgeon immediately. The post-mortem later found Thomas's sword had penetrated both ventricles of Branthwaite's heart.

Describing the events leading up to the fateful encounter, Thomas explained to the Old Bailey judge that he had been placed in an impossible situation. As he accompanied Branthwaite to Charing-Cross in the coach his accuser became increasingly agitated. He 'fell in a violent Passion, and told me that I had acted like a Rascal and a Scoundrel' in regard to some 'affair of great consequence'. Branthwaite complained Thomas had also besmirched his character in another business matter. At that point Branthwaite had shown him the duelling pistols and threatened to shoot him there and then if he tried to leave the coach.

Thomas was at pains to explain that he had been an unwilling participant in the events that played out in Hyde Park, and several 'persons of distinction' gave him the 'character of being a Gentleman of a very agreeable even Temper, not in the least inclinable to be quarrelsome.' It was a persuasive enough argument for the judge who found him guilty of a lesser charge: manslaughter.

Sentences were later imposed on all the convicted villains from the court sessions of that month. Thirty four were transported, one was 'whipt' and fifteen others were sentenced to death. One woman was to be 'drawn on a Hurdle, to the Place of Execution, and there to be burnt.' Thomas's punishment was in the more lenient category favoured by judges in cases regarded merely as gentlemen's disagreements. He was sentenced to branding, or burning in the hand. Certainly this must have been a relief to his wife Julian, then three months pregnant with their first child, Berney.

Berney probably spent his childhood privately tutored at his family home in Great Baddow, near Chelmsford in Essex. In April 1744 at the age of seventeen he began his university education at Trinity Hall, Cambridge. The following year, having recently received a timely legacy of twenty guineas from his aunt Jemima Branthwaite specifically to buy himself a watch, he was admitted to Lincoln's Inn to begin his law studies. But unlike his younger brother (Thomas, named after their father) he did not pursue this career, although he did pursue justice when he discovered some of his clothes had been stolen during a stay in London in 1746.

By this time he was a twenty-year-old independent man-about-town. During his prosecution at the Old Bailey of Anna Maria Leverstone for theft and grand larceny, he told the court that he had come 'up to London, and took Lodgings at Mr. Egleston's, Tobacconist in Fleet-Street'. In fact he had actually gone *down* to London from Chelmsford, but this was just one of those little class-related nuances of speech which decreed that there were only two cities in Britain to which one could "go up", namely London and Edinburgh, regardless of where you were travelling from.

He continued: 'I pack'd up my Things in a Portmanteau to go in the Country: After I had been in the Country about three Weeks, I look'd for some of my Pocket Handkerchiefs, and I miss'd them; I miss'd three Shirts and five Handkerchiefs.' At the time of leaving his lodgings Berney had been distracted by a visit from his brother Thomas – also studying law in London – who had arrived to accompany him home to Great Baddow.

Berney had instructed the maid, Anna Leverstone, to leave the room while he did his own packing, and he inadvertently left out the items he later missed. After he left, the opportunistic Miss Leverstone decided she had as much right to Berney's clothes as her employer, and promptly pawned them for a total of eighteen shillings. She was found guilty and sentenced to transportation for seven years.

Berney wasn't cut out to be a lawyer like his brother. While Thomas continued his law studies Berney decided a military life would suit him better. In February 1747 the London press announced that on presentation to King George II by General Folliot, Berney was appointed ensign in the 1st Regiment of Foot Guards.

Four and a half years pass before we find notice of him again, when in October 1751 he had 'lately arrived from his travels [and] kissed his Majesty's hand' on his appointment as Captain of the Grenadiers, under William, Duke of Cumberland, the king's younger son. The implication here is that he had probably been away in Europe on the Grand Tour, during which he may have either broadened his horizons and improved his manners, or engaged in gambling, profligacy and debauchery, a common accusation levelled at the privileged sons of 18th century Gentlemen. The latter might seem a more likely fit for his character.

Two years later in April 1753 Berney's father died at Great Baddow. He left him a portfolio of real estate in Norfolk, including the coastal manors of Horsey and Waxham, and also the great tithes and 100 acres of glebe at Aldbury, Hertfordshire, thus raising his status considerably. In addition to these inheritances he became heir-at-law to the remnants left by his foolish cousin, Sir Thomas Brograve of Hamels, 3rd Baronet, an accidental heir who had spent extravagantly and dissipated most of his inheritance.

But there would be no time yet for marriage and peaceful enjoyment of his newly acquired wealth. The antagonism between the British Empire and their adversaries in Europe was a hot topic in Parliament, and Berney now had a vested interest in defending British soil against enemy invaders. The conflict which became known as The Seven Years' War began with a formal declaration by Britain against France in mid-May 1756, and with a French invasion a distinct possibility, the Militia Bill was introduced in the Commons in January the following year.

The Militia Act established Militia Regiments in all counties of England and Wales. George Townshend (Viscount Townshend from 1764 and 1st Marquis Townshend from 1787) was instrumental in its formation in Norfolk. Berney would later regard Townshend as a friend.

The training of local men was also enthusiastically supported by Townshend's kinsman and neighbour William Windham (later Secretary of War) who compiled an elaborate drill book with an introduction and sketches by Townshend, entitled: *A Plan of Discipline for the Use of the Norfolk Militia*. Berney retired from the regular army and joined the Eastern Battalion of the Norfolk Militia under the command of George Walpole, Lord Orford.

As a new member of the Militia Berney was obliged under the Test Act of 1673 to take the oaths of supremacy and allegiance, a religious test which imposed various civil disabilities on Roman Catholics and Nonconformists. Only those professing the Established Church were eligible for civil or military office. He was required to make an oath and declaration that he fulfilled the requirement of receiving the sacrament according to Anglican rites.

His militia officer's uniform was an elaborate affair. It reflected the superior wealth and social status of men drawn from the ranks of the aristocracy and gentry, whereas the origins of regular army officers tended to be more from the middle classes. The fact that a militia officer was unlikely to spoil his uniform on active service also allowed a certain amount of extra creativity in their design. Based on sketches in Windham's drill book, Berney would have looked very smart in his scarlet single breasted coat carrying a fusil[2] and bayonet. Completing the ensemble were buff-coloured breeches and waistcoat with white stockings inside black leather boots.

Berney's inherited property was kept tenanted in his absence, and during the course of the next few years he criss-crossed the country. In November 1758 he was in Norwich celebrating the king's birthday with his fellow officers, and seven months later their regiment was in Portsmouth, at that time the first of any Militia group to leave their home county. They continued on to London and amid cheering crowds, passing in review before George II at Kensington. The king asked Orford the names of the officers as they passed, doffing his hat to each in turn. Six months later Berney was in charge of thirty militia recruits. Under a direct order from the Secretary of War, having paid them a guinea each as required by an Act of Parliament, he sent them on a march to Gloucestershire to join their new regiment.

In July 1760 Berney commanded two companies of Norfolk Militia quartered at Great Yarmouth, guarding French prisoners. There had been a recent history of escapes. After a furious sea-battle off Winterton in 1754 between *H.M.S. Hazard* and the French privateer *La Subtille*, 86 French prisoners had been lodged in the jail. Fourteen escaped by undermining part of the prison wall and only four were recaptured. No lesson had been learned in the interim and just prior to Berney's arrival at Yarmouth twenty-eight prisoners had also escaped by the same method. By the time he got there all but three had been recaptured. His regiment was relieved after a month and marched back to Norwich to await further orders.

Marriage, Family, and the Sweet Smell of... Effluvia??

The battle for territorial supremacy continued to rage in Europe but with the anticipated French invasion averted, a relieved Berney was now in a position to consider his future. In May 1761 he was married at Great Baddow. His new bride was Jane, the eldest of three daughters of Edward Hawker of Great Baddow and his wife Elizabeth Hall. According to *The History and Antiquities of the County of Essex* written not long afterwards, the Brograves and Hawkers were 'families of fashion' in the neighbourhood, and probably friends of longstanding.

Edward Hawker had died five years earlier leaving Jane his house Noakes Place in Great Baddow (demolished 1968) and other property, subject to the life interest of her mother. Only a year after Jane's marriage to Berney her mother also died, allowing possession to pass to Berney in right of his wife. He retained ownership of Noakes Place until 1785 when he sold it together with Brick Farm and a quantity of felled timber from the estate. The death of Berney's mother-in-law added a little more to his fortune materially, but misfortune lurked just around the corner.

The manor of Waxham and the adjoining manor of Horsey had been purchased in 1733 by his father from Thomas Blofield under an order of the Court of Chancery. Just over three decades later Berney added to his patrimony thanks to another Chancery decree which allowed him to purchase the manor of Palling - which also adjoined Waxham - together with shipwreck salvage rights, the great tithes and perpetual advowson of the church. Berney's ownership of these three manors would prove to be a mixed blessing.

Despite Waxham church being on his estate, all of Berney and Jane's children were baptised at St. Mary's, Worstead. Their first daughter Julian Elizabeth was born just before Easter 1762, followed the next year by twin girls, Anne and Susannah; the latter dying within a week. His son and would-be heir Berney Hall Brograve was born less than two years later but survived only three weeks.

Within three months of that child's death Berney's wife was also dead. It was now August 1765 and in the space of little more than four years he had gone from being a hopeful newly-wed to a widower, having also lost two of his four children, the survivors now aged two and three years. This must surely have seemed like the worst time of his life.

With yet another funeral to arrange, 38 year-old Berney was a familiar figure at Worstead's beautiful 14th century church. The church at Waxham, St. John's, is of even greater antiquity, mentioned in the Domesday Book when it was compiled in A.D. 1086. It is located close to Waxham Hall but like all members of Berney's family, Jane was not buried there.

Within a month of her death Berney placed an announcement in the *Norwich Mercury:* '...wanted by me a middle aged woman who perfectly understands cooking and a table; she is likewise to act as housekeeper; she must not be wasteful ...' This last prerequisite, while desirable in a housekeeper, perhaps hints at another of Berney's character traits.

The winter of 1765-6 was particularly severe, and as the weather closed in he must have felt acutely the gloom and isolation that engulfed his death-ravaged household. With events still painfully fresh in his mind, during the following year he arranged to have a proper entrance built to access the Brograve burial vault at Worstead.

Two years passed, giving Berney time to consider his next move. He renewed his lease at Worstead and started building a new house there while continuing to farm at Waxham, about ten miles distant as the crow flies.

He maintained a congenial relationship with Lord and Lady Townshend. They had sent him a present of a buck in the summer of 1768 for which he returned a note of thanks,[3] but rather than write it himself he had delegated this task to someone in his household at Worstead. The careful choice of wording by Berney's diplomatic intermediary-cum-social secretary gives the impression that he, or perhaps it was his wife, would have been a particularly valuable asset to a man of rather unpredictable temperament - as Berney would prove to be as time went on.

Berney's best compliments were presented to Lord and Lady Townshend, and 'He thinks himself extremely obliged to his Lordship for his Present of a Buck; and that he is very much honored by receiving at the same time so polite a Card'. The writer conveyed Berney's hope that it would not be long before he would have the satisfaction of 'making his bow to his Excellency' on this side of the water.

Dividing his time between two estates meant Berney occasionally frustrated visitors by his absence if they arrived unexpectedly, as one William Hardy discovered. He had gone to Worstead to inspect one of Berney's properties, the Kings Head Inn, but was disappointed to find him not at home. Mrs. Hardy notes that 'Mr. Hart hired the Kings Head at Worstead of Mr. Brograve, came & agreed to take beer of Mr. Hardy.'[4]

The records show that Berney was not a particularly benevolent landlord. Nevertheless, with land ownership there were social obligations. While he was obliged to honour certain charities related to his vested estates, Berney also occasionally contributed voluntarily to causes such as the hospital at Norwich. These gestures were few and far between however, and insufficient to dispel the notion that he was a miserly squire.

His objection to the amount assessed on his land in Worstead for the poor rate only reinforced the perception. Between 1764 and

1769 all landowners in the parish paid their assessed rate except Berney. Aggrieved by what he deemed an unfair system of assessment, he informed the churchwardens and overseers that if the rates were not altered, he would not abide by them. This blunt refusal would probably have been made in such an intimidating manner as to make any negotiation impossible.

The churchwardens took him to court where he submitted an appeal complaining of the inequity of the rates. Houses were assessed at half their annual value and land at three quarters. The magistrates were unanimous in dismissing his argument, thereby setting the benchmark for future poor rate assessment (for a long time afterwards *Rex v. Brograve* has been frequently cited in similar court cases). Berney was ordered to pay up.

He gained no sympathy for another grievance he took to the Court of Exchequer in 1772 (*Brograve v. Mace*) when he accused two of his tenants at Worstead of defrauding him of his tithes. He complained they were loading up their wagons with the sheaves of wheat and removing the nine parts of the crop before he could make any judgement as to whether they had left him a fair tenth, and by the time the gleaners and cattle had been in the field there was nothing much left of it anyway.

No doubt their quick getaway was designed to prevent an altercation, but when he was angry Berney was a difficult man to avoid. The defendants said he had 'harassed and distressed' them, and they maintained it was Berney's responsibility to safeguard his tenth. The court agreed and dismissed the case, ordering him to pay costs. Worstead's poor, 2: Bernie, nil.

Four years after the death of his wife, Berney was ready to try his luck again. At Hoe near East Dereham, an energetic south-westward gallop from Worstead of twenty three miles, he found himself a young heiress just 12 months before she inherited her father's estates. He was slightly more than twice her age, and in January 1769 at the age of 43 Berney married another Jane, the daughter of Matthew Halcott. Halcott was one of several successive generations who had made their wealth from hide tanning at nearby Litcham.

Jane brought to the marriage estates in Beeston and Litcham, each vested with a rent charge to benefit their poor inhabitants. In 1679 John Halcott had given an almshouse at Litcham for '2 poor ancient men to dwell in' with an endowment of ten pounds per annum charged on the property later held by Berney, and at Beeston the rent charge of three pounds per annum was distributed in bread to the poor at the parish church every Sunday.

Over the next fourteen years Berney and the second Mrs. Jane Brograve produced a further thirteen children: seven daughters and six sons. Beginning in December 1769 the first ten of these were baptised at Worstead. The last three, Roger, Dorothy and Matthew, were baptised at St. John's, Waxham. The continuation of the line was assured; there was an heir and plenty of 'spares'. Or so it seemed. Despite the high rate of fertility there was never room for complacency. The rate of infant mortality was also high and Berney would be an unwitting contributor to the inconvenient situation of "failure of issue".

In a painfully familiar sequence of events, the first of Berney's second round of "failures" began with Margaret and her sister Jane, who both died in April 1772 aged one year, buried on the same day. Charlotte died three years later aged six, followed by nine month-old Jemima less than a year afterwards. Three years later one year-old Edward died, and then another daughter also named Jane six weeks later.

The thirteen year respite before the next series of losses might have given Berney and his wife a false sense of security. Beginning in March 1792 the death occurred of his eldest daughter from his first marriage, Julian Elizabeth (then Mrs. Thomas Gregory), who had given birth to her only child two months earlier. Just a few weeks later her half-sister, fifteen year-old Carolyn also died. Death cut a further swathe through the Brograve family in the following months. Early in 1793 twelve-year old Dorothy died, followed by Berney's wife Jane eight weeks later, aged 45. Twenty-year-old Thomas died the day after his mother. All but two of these deaths occurred during the months of March, April and May, coinciding with storms and flooding at Berney's estate at Waxham.

The indiscriminate nature of death meant life for rich and poor alike was a precarious affair. The uncertain future faced by every newborn child was tempered somewhat by the practice of having large families to ensure a successor, and Berney's wives had little choice but to accept their lot and keep up a steady supply. Nothing is known of these two women. It could be said that perhaps the first Jane was the more fortunate of the two, having only lived four years as his wife. Her successor endured twenty-four years, during which Berney notoriously alienated their friends and neighbours, abused and scared off his workers, and may well have also frightened her and their unfortunate progeny out of their wits on a regular basis.

Regardless of the sufferings of his family, it is Berney who is remembered for his ill-temper and intemperate habits. Perhaps this could be interpreted as a manifestation of unresolved grief, given the numbers and frequency of bereavement. The last five deaths in just two years decimated the family, leaving him with one daughter Anne from his first marriage, and four sons from the second. Of these sons, the eldest at 21 was George, and his younger brothers John, 17, Roger, 13, and Matthew, 10. These last three were also destined to die premature and tragic deaths.

It is a high mortality rate for a single family, even by eighteenth century standards. Just twenty miles away influenza was reported as raging through the population of Norwich in 1775, and smallpox had long been an indiscriminate scourge. Many wealthier families attempted to prevent it by inoculation, but an unfortunate side effect was sometimes death from the small dose they were given. Others who were inoculated became carriers of the disease, transmitting it to people they came into contact with.

The killer of Berney's family was more likely to have have been malaria, endemic in England in the eighteenth century, and thought to emanate from effluvia or "bad air". Geographic areas with large tracts of low-lying land and many slow-flowing or stagnant stretches of water, such as those in close proximity to Waxham Hall, were ideal for the spread of the insect-borne virus. It was prevalent in the summer in East Anglia with its many marshes, broads and fens. 1792 was a particularly bad year for flooding and "bad air" at Waxham. The deaths of Berney's wife and children in the year between March 1792 and March 1793 occurred after nine separate floods during 1792, which lasted until December of that year.

---

[2] A light flintlock musket
[3] N.R.O Ref BL/T/8/2/26
[4] Mary Hardy's Diary, p127, by Mary Hardy, B. Cozens-Hardy, 1968

Chapter 3
A Target of Criticism and Cannonballs

Berney felt very vulnerable at Waxham, teetering on the edge of the unprotected coast. As well as the constantly encroaching sea there remained the real possibility of a French invasion. He detested the French. And he detested smugglers. The feeling was mutual.

The many tales of hauntings in the area were probably a tactic used by smugglers to keep the frightened locals in at night whilst the boats landed and distributed their contraband. The gullible villagers were particularly fearful of the Black Shuck, an enormous ghostly dog. To encounter the fire-breathing apparition with its single glowing eye was said to be an omen of death before the year was out.

The smuggling activities reached a peak in the mid 1770's despite attempts at intervention by revenue cutters sent to patrol the coast. Although they were a familiar sight, their efforts met with mixed success. Occasionally goods were seized and the offenders hanged, but for the most part the smugglers managed to stay one step ahead of the law and two steps ahead of Berney.

From time to time reluctant participants were rounded up and pressed into gangs by armed men. The smugglers often hid their vessels in the reeds at Horsey under cover of darkness – on Berney's land – before transporting the contraband inland. They were confident and elusive, and on one occasion in 1775 when one of their number was caught, a group of armed men intercepted the post-chaise on its way to Norwich Castle, threatening to shoot the guards if they did not immediately release their prisoner. Some were not so lucky, such as James Carbold, (alias Jiffling Jack) and Charles Gowen, (alias the Papist of Beccles), who were both outlawed in 1749 and executed a year later.

In 1751 it had been reported that the headquarters of a band of armed smugglers was located on Berney's adjoining property at Palling where they had a secret vault to hide the contraband. Probably what rankled Berney the most was that it was happening virtually under his nose. Employing no bailiff to help manage his farm he was powerless to stop it. Nor could he rally any local support. He simply could not be everywhere at once, and despite his reputation for bravado he was not so foolish as to venture out alone in the dark to confront a band of armed men. While the animosity between Berney and the smugglers escalated, other landowners either turned a blind eye or willingly assisted, and some used their mill sails to signal the smuggler's vessel when the coast was clear.

A journalist from the *Norfolk Chronicle* gave his opinion on the subject in an article dated September 1783:

> "Tis remarkable, from experience, that smuggling and poaching are the beginning and foundation of almost every other capital crime, besides the very great injury done to the fair trader. Notwithstanding this fact is so well known, the encouragement given to these sort of idle

and disorderly persons by different ranks of people is astonishing and truly alarming! The acquittal of a very notorious smuggler at last Thetford assizes is one instance fresh in the memory of numbers of people, and what rejoicings were made at particular places on account of such acquittal. The consequences arising therefrom are to be dreaded by every sober person; and therefore, surely, 'tis worthy of one of the first consideration of our Legislators to contrive some law more effectual to bring such offenders to justice, and strictly to put those laws in execution already made, which greatly want a revisal and digestion."

Generally speaking, public sentiment against government taxation has changed little over the centuries, but there is little doubt Berney would have been in complete agreement with the journalist's stance against smugglers and their supporters. While not altogether a 'sober person' all of the time, he was nevertheless aware of the consequences of his anti-smuggling attitude. He was prepared to risk making himself even more unpopular by doing all he could to suppress the illegal trade.

He would have fully supported his old regiment, the Eastern battalion of the Norfolk militia. They had engaged smugglers in a longboat in July 1778 while it was unloading on shore, but the villains managed to reach their schooner. They fired on the militia from their superior vantage point and made good their escape.

To draw attention to the situation now almost out of control, a petition was presented in the House of Commons six months after this incident. The possibility of removing the duty on tea was raised as a means of preventing the temptation. The earlier anti-smuggling bill which had been passed in 1736 at the instigation of legitimate traders had little beneficial effect in the interim, and as far as being a deterrent, it was not worth the paper it was printed on. Subsequent legislation also failed.

It was no less rampant in the early nineteenth century. Rev. Henry Ready, Rector of Waxham-cum-Palling for nearly sixty years, wrote that when he first arrived at Waxham he was advised by the outgoing incumbent that if he were to find a keg of brandy by his front door it meant his barn was being used by smugglers, and he must keep away strangers. He was instructed to check every day and when a second keg appeared on his doorstep he would know that all was clear. The barn referred to was Berney's Great Barn, contiguous to Waxham Hall and St. John's church, built in 1583-4 and now celebrated as the largest surviving historic barn in Norfolk.

Waxham Great Barn in 1992 before restoration
Photo copyright George Plunkett

A Slightly Exaggerated Report

At the height of the smuggling problem in mid-April 1779 several houses Berney owned in the village of Palling were destroyed by fire.[5] It may have appeared accidental, but more likely it was the beginning of a campaign of retribution by the smugglers, designed to dampen Berney's enthusiasm. By this time he had become so unpopular that in September, just over four months after the torching, an unknown person notified the London press that he had died at Waxham the previous Friday. While he'd undoubtedly had more than his fair share of fights and hangovers, none had so far proved fatal. The revelation that he had suddenly passed away at the age of 53 would certainly have been news to Berney.

The announcement appeared in at least five London newspapers and a monthly magazine, convincing not only the general public but also his three siblings who had no immediate access to the true facts. The unexpected news of his death may have been eclipsed by an even more startling revelation: his uncharacteristic generosity. The press reported that he had left 'considerable benefactions to public charities, and appointed Sir Harbord Harbord sole executor'.[6] It appears the smugglers had a sense of humour.

The selection of executor seemed perfectly plausible, since Sir Harbord, M.P for Norwich (created Baron Suffield in 1786), was probably a friend - or an acquaintance at the very least. They had mutual property dealings, and Harbord's daughter Catherine later married one of Berney's cousins. The addition of Harbord's name certainly lends credibility to the report, suggesting a well-informed enemy with a more intimate knowledge of Berney's affairs and associates.

For seventeen days the world believed Berney was dead – until the *St. James's Chronicle* sheepishly published a retraction. They were careful not to accept the entire blame: 'The Report of the Death of B. Brograve Esq., inferred in this and other News-Papers, is groundless, that Gentleman being in perfect Health.' Perfect presumably, only inasmuch as he was still alive with plenty of fight left, since Berney wasn't in the best physical shape. One of his few pleasures was eating. The other of course was drinking, and plenty of it, so by this time his liver and other internal organs might have told a different story to the version the *Chronicle* would have its readers believe.

As far as anonymous death threats went this was certainly pernicious, but as a deterrent it had failed. It was much too subtle to intimidate Berney; he became all the more determined. Still fuming at their audacity he continued his campaign. But the smugglers were just as determined to prevent him from ruining their livelihoods and it wouldn't be long before he would receive yet another payback for his interference.

In January 1780 the London papers reported that Berney was again in the firing line, this time the target of well-aimed cannon. The inhabitants of Horsey, Palling and Waxham, and needless to say Bernie too, were greatly alarmed by the sound of cannon-fire during the night when a passing vessel fired several shots at Waxham Hall.

The discovery of cannonballs around the house the next morning confirmed it. Although no damage was done to his property it had put fear into Bernie's heart. So much so, in fact, he would still be complaining about the incident fourteen years later in a letter to Lord Townshend.

The house was a relatively close target for the smugglers' cannons but when it was originally constructed in the 16th century it was said to be some fourteen miles from the sea. This may or may not be an exaggeration nurtured by locals and the passing of time. Certainly large chunks of the coast have disappeared. There were once two medieval villages: Waxham Magna and Waxham Parva. The latter was located a third of a mile to the north-east before it was lost to the sea, and since then the ongoing erosion has resulted in Waxham Hall being now only about 200 yards from the edge of the water.

Regardless of the coastline crumbling bit by bit around them, the local population had no sympathy for Berney. It may possibly have given them some secret satisfaction knowing he had the most to lose; he owned every marsh, field and cottage as far as the eye could see, and along with maritime disasters came rich pickings. But despite his legal rights to shipwreck salvage Berney had competition from opportunistic locals, the villagers often looting them before he could secure any cargo.

In 1768 they swooped on the *Lady Agatha* when she was wrecked off Sea Palling. Perhaps taking advantage of Berney's absence and preoccupation with his newly-built house at Worstead, they plundered cargo worth fifty thousand pounds which was never recovered. On another occasion after a storm on New Year's Eve in 1779 eleven ships were washed ashore and immediately plundered. The local population behaved 'more like savages than civilised people', according to the *Norwich Mercury*.[7]

Unable to prevent the pillage, one might imagine Berney's first reaction when he ran onto the beach was to wave his arms and bellow into the wind. Hoping to attract more attention after a particularly efficient dispersal of cargo in 1789 he inserted a carefully worded notice in the Norwich newspaper. He warned the 'many persons' who had purloined goods or effects from the wreck that it was a felony under an Act of Parliament. He would proceed against them with the utmost rigour of the law.

Inevitably Berney was a target for thieves. The *Norfolk Chronicle* reported in 1783 there was a gang operating in the neighbourhood. His stable at Waxham had been 'entered by some villains' who stole three leather cart collars and several other articles, but were never caught. A few weeks later one of the gang, Robert Turner of Martham, was found guilty of stealing three sacks of wheat from Berney's barn, fined one shilling and sentenced to two years hard labour in London's Bridewell prison.

The following year a horse was taken which Berney said was 'something of the running strain'. Just after dark on another night, one of his cart horses was stolen. Earlier that evening a man was seen loitering in the lane outside the stable. Berney described him as round shouldered, mid-thirties, 'stoops very much in his walk, speaks very hoarse' with dark lank hair. His description of the stolen horse indicates the unfortunate beast didn't have a particularly easy life either. 'A small black horse of the Punch breed… his mouth is very much cut by the halter; both sides chafed with the harness; when rid, carries his head out, and badly.' He promised a reward of ten guineas, over and above the finder's entitlement of forty pounds by Act of Parliament.

Not everyone was intent on taking advantage of Berney. He received an anonymous letter from "A Friend" informing him he was being 'daily robb'd at Worstead'. Robert Watts, who leased the public house at Worstead from Berney, had stolen a sack marked 'B. Brograve, Waxham' and some straw from his farmyard. Berney took him to court.

Witnesses corroborated Berney's evidence but somehow Watts convinced the jury of his innocence. Berney was not able to let the injustice pass. Hoping for more information to secure a conviction he inserted a notice in the press offering a reward to the anonymous 'friend' who wrote the letter. The amount was again ten guineas, a worthwhile sum of money to the average person at the time. As time went by his rewards became less valuable. It was later five guineas for information leading to the conviction of the thief who entered his granary via a window and stole a sack of wheat.

Despite the majority of stories relating to Berney being centred at Waxham, a later tenant of the Hall mentions nothing about the legends of ghosts or bloodstained walls in 1854, little more than fifty years after his death. The impression of Berney given by the tenant was one of benign benevolence when one Daniel Gurney of Runcton visited the Hall. 'He farmed his own land, and had about a hundred workmen lodging in his house; these all dined in the great hall together, and Sir Berney every now and then "knocked down" a bullock for them to live upon.'[8]

Gurney also makes the claim that 'He was the last gentleman who kept a fool.' There were still private fools in the early 18th century (Swift wrote an epitaph on Dicky Pearce, the Earl of Suffolk's jester who died c.1725), although this may have been stretching the timeline somewhat to include Berney. Or it may have been a confused version of the story that a former owner of Waxham Hall, Sir William Woodhouse, was supposedly jester to James I.

In the absence of any known physical portrait, perhaps a more accurate picture is provided by one of Berney's contemporaries, William Marshall, who visited him at Waxham in 1782. In his book on the rural economy of Norfolk,[9] Marshall describes the agriculture and land management of the county, naming several farmers in the area. Berney receives a special mention, although not explicitly by name. He is referred to in the first instance as 'Mr. B____e', possibly a half-hearted attempt at protecting his subject's identity, although more likely for Marshall's own bodily well-being since he published his book in Berney's lifetime.

In the event that Berney had read this publication he would hardly have failed to recognise himself; Marshall also mentions that 'Mr. B.' is the owner of Waxham and Horsey. Although its purpose was to inform the reader of such things as local soil conditions and farming practices, it is a good indication of Berney's notoriety that Marshall goes out of his way to describe his peculiarities:

> "The character of this man is so very extraordinary, that I cannot refrain from sketching some of its principal features. He was, I believe, bred in the army; served some time in the militia; has fought two or three duels; quarrelled with most of the gentlemen of the county; and, coming to a good paternal estate, discharged his tenants and commenced farmer. He is now an occupier of seventeen hundred pounds a year - yet he has neither steward nor even bailiff to assist him: no wonder, then, he abuses and receives abuse from his work-people; or that he sometimes frightens them away; his harvest, perhaps, standing still, until his neighbours have finished. He attends fairs and markets - fells his own corn and his own bullocks; and even finds time to attend to the taking in gift stock upon a very extensive marsh - and this without any assistance; save that of his lady, who keeps his accounts.
>
> My fellow traveller being acquainted with him, we rode through his farm yard, and found him looking over some young cattle which had been brought up for his inspection. His person is gross, and his appearance bacchanalian - his dress that of a slovenly gentleman. There is a politeness in his manner; and his conversation

bespeaks a sensible intelligent mind; borne away, however, by a wildness and ferocity which is obvious in his countenance, and discovers itself in every word and action. Nevertheless, it is said, that, in a polite circle, Mr. B. *can* excel in politeness."

This apparently well-measured description conveys quite a vivid picture. Berney seems to fit a certain stereotype on which many writers of fiction have modelled a particularly unlikeable character. For example, there are obvious similarities between Berney's quirky attributes and William Makepeace Thackeray's Sir Pitt Crawley in *Vanity Fair*, a boisterous, bitter and mean-spirited baronet who was often drunk and beat his wife. Not that there is any evidence that Berney was also a wife-beater in addition to his other "interesting" traits, but certainly no one would have envied any spouse of his.

While everywhere men drank prodigiously, Marshall's 'bacchanalian' description implies that Berney's alcohol consumption was a well-entrenched ritual, a trait often mentioned in stories about him. His apparently slovenly appearance was perhaps a by-product of his liberal self-medication. In an age of polish and refinement Berney was hardly a paragon of taste - unlike his eminent contemporary Lord Chesterfield, renowned for his pedantic grooming, meticulous dress and manners. To be fair, Berney was a hands-on farmer receiving unexpected visitors that day and it would have been impractical to attire himself in anything which might be spoiled by mud and manure.

The grossness of his person probably meant his middle-aged corpulence would no longer fit into the dashing militia uniform of his youth. The result of excessive drinking and over-eating - two classic ingredients in a recipe for disaster of the bodily kind - must have been obvious to Marshall. The physical abuse and neglect Berney had lavished on himself for so many years would indicate that he was long past the point of no return. Marshall's description eloquently illustrates Berney's decline in the fourteen years since 1768 when he was still active in Lord Townshend's social circle and on the lookout for a new wife after the untimely death of the first.

The fact that he had no steward or bailiff in 1782 suggests reluctance on his part to relinquish control of certain aspects of his farm management, but his notoriously argumentative temperament might have been sufficient deterrent for a prospective bailiff considering the position. That Berney had any workers at all would have been due to their pressing need of income to feed the numerous hungry mouths at home. Little wonder then that some of the locals preferred the lucrative occupation of smuggling rather than a lowly-paid tongue-lashing from Berney.

But despite Marshall's implication that Berney had a high turnover of workers, he did have at least one faithful and trusty servant, the thick-skinned John Leach. He began with Berney as a young lad and remained loyal to him for twenty years till the death of his master, and continued in the service of Berney's son George for another thirty years. Leach outlived both father and son - dying at the ripe old age of 82 in 1844.

It becomes apparent that for all his faults Berney did have at least one redeeming feature: he was not afraid of hard work. While many of his peers revelled in self-indulgence, he was not a typical eighteenth century society gentleman - idly rich - who saw no point in squandering energy and whose leisure hours amounted to 24 a day. There were others who, without forgoing their normal pleasures of drinking and gambling, might electrify parliament with some profound pronouncement, or otherwise contribute something worthy to the world of literature.

Berney didn't fit that particular stereotype. As he got older he courted society only when it suited his purpose. He was prepared to get his hands dirty - whether by choice or necessity - and his tight-fisted reputation was well-known. As Marshall pointed out: 'Mr. B. does not injure his fortune by farming, for it seems generally allowed that no farmer gets his work done as cheap as Mr. B.'

While not particularly impressed with the man or his appearance, Marshall was surprisingly generous in his praise of Berney's farming expertise. He describes his land as 'rich and fertile in a high degree', from which he harvested 'exceedingly fine crops' despite 'the irregularity with which his affairs are conducted'. Compared to Berney's reluctant and abused workers and overworked horses, his livestock had a rather more leisurely existence, floods and slaughter notwithstanding.

According to Marshall, his animals had free egress to the sea, 'on the edge of which they delight to lie in the heat of the summer when they lie cool and free from the flies, with which the marshes are greatly pestered.' Berney's nearest neighbour, who rented an adjoining marsh from him, was compelled to erect faggot-fences between the sand hills and the beach to prevent the intermingling of his stock with Berney's, thus avoiding the unpleasant repercussions that would otherwise inevitably ensue.

---

[5] History and Antiquities of the County of Norfolk, Vol.7
[6] Morning Post and Daily Advertiser (London), Sept 9, 1779; Issue 2154, amongst others
[7] Palling - A History Shaped by the Sea, Pestell R, 1986, Poppyland.
[8] The Record of the House of Gournay - Page 776, Daniel Gurney - 1858
[9] The Rural Economy of Norfolk: Comprising The Management Of Landed Estates, And The Present Practice Of Husbandry In That County" Vol II, William Marshall 1795

Chapter 4
Sir Berney's Battle with the Sea

Despite his life punctuated by the loss of so many children and both his wives, not to mention the antagonism he encountered on a personal level, the ruination of Berney's land by seawater presented an ongoing and insurmountable problem. The coast along his three adjoining manors is about twenty miles north of Lowestoft, the most eastern part of Britain. It is also very low-lying and in many places below the level of spring tides. Under James I an Act had been passed in 1608 after severe damage caused by 'violent inundations'. Commissioners were appointed to keep the defences in good repair, but over a period of time the action of gale-force winds and pounding waves overwhelmed their efforts.

In addition to repeated flooding, the large numbers of vessels which have come to grief on that part of the storm-prone coast caused much loss of life. During one infamous event in 1703 three hundred ships were wrecked. Twenty years later - when Berney was still just a twinkle in his father's eye, writer Daniel Defoe described it as the most dangerous coast in Britain, and accordingly he had his character Robinson Crusoe wrecked off East Anglia on his first voyage.

While the disastrous combination of very high tides and strong north-westerly gales frequently wreak havoc on the Norfolk coastline, the Norfolk Broads is also an area of great natural beauty. On a fine day under a blue velvet sky the broad levels of marshland shimmer in the sun, extending inland in defiance of the constant human effort to reclaim them. For Berney the need to drain his waterlogged land took his mind off smugglers and the despicable French temporarily; having large areas of stagnant water in his backyard was simply unproductive – not to mention, unhealthy. In 1771 he set about building a wind pump and a series of drainage ditches through an area known as Brograve Level to create a grazing marsh.

Originally wind-driven, Brograve Mill changed to steam power in 1850. Standing starkly against the picturesque landscape, the mill is now derelict and leans at a slight angle to the west. The reason for this, according to folklore, once again involves Berney and the devil. As the story goes, the devil was furious with Berney for having the audacity to reclaim some of his flooded land, and tried to blow it down. Obviously it was built too well and all he could manage was a little subsidence, which in the Norfolk dialect would be described as being distinctly 'on the huh'.

Over the centuries the forces of nature have considerably changed the topography of the East Anglian coast, and there are many recorded instances of houses, inns and churches lost to the encroaching waves. Waxham was once a considerable village with large tracts of cultivated land extending eastwards into what was then called the German Ocean (now the North Sea).

Just north of Palling, the Eccles church tower - originally some distance from the shore, had stood on the beach slowly disintegrating for about a century. In 1839, when geologist Sir Charles Lyell visited Norfolk, the tower was half-buried in the sand-hills and at one time it was possible to walk in and out of its belfry window. The tower was still standing in 1887, but by 1938 only two large fragments protruded from the sand, the rest having succumbed to the same fate as the village that once surrounded it.

Today, the long serrated line of Marram-covered sand hills extending from Palling to Horsey is the only barrier between Waxham Hall and the sea, and although of some height, their soft sandy slopes lack substance and breadth. During every exceptionally high tide tons of sand are scoured away. Even when his land was not under water, Berney must have been all too aware of the slowly diminishing distance between the gatehouse at Waxham and the waves lapping ever closer.

In 1781 there were many breaches in the six mile stretch between Waxham and Winterton which destroyed some of his crops, a house was washed away and the drinking water contaminated. When William Marshall visited him in a few months later, Berney told him that he had 'four acres of very fine cole-seed swept down during the late tempestuous weather.'[10] The following year, in November 1782, four vessels were driven ashore at Eccles, Palling and Waxham during a storm. Also found washed up on Berney's beach amongst the flotsam was a strange and mysterious creature.

Much of what lurked in the uncharted depths was still unknown, and no one knew quite what to make of it. The animal, 'not yet described by naturalists', was about 5ft 10" in length, 4ft in circumference with 'four legs and paws' and had joints in the hind legs, giving rise to speculation that 'it occasionally sits upright like a baboon'. With a large round head, broad back and prominent belly, it 'on the whole, resembles a porpus, more than any Sea Production we have seen'.[11]

A decade or so earlier, an attempt had been made to make some sense of the natural world. George Edwards of the Royal Society made the following rather unedifying statement: 'Quadrupeds seem to unite with fishes; for it is doubtful whether we should class the several species of the Seal kind with the four-footed beasts or fishes: they are hairy, and have teeth like four-footed beasts; but, whether to call their extremities feet or fins, with propriety, I do not know'. The earlier gusto of the Royal Society which had characterised its research and experiments in the seventeenth century had all but stagnated in the eighteenth, and twenty-two years later still no knowledge had been gained to identify the large four-legged 'fish' on Berney's beach.

The sea breaches remained open for the next sixteen years. This would prove a nightmare for Berney, who had been vigorously pressing for reparation of the sea embankment at the joint expense of landowners under a Commission of Sewers. The continual refusal by the majority of landowners had long frustrated him. He told William Marshall nearly a decade earlier that 'it is not for me to attack the German Ocean single-handed'.[12]

There appeared some hope on the horizon in July 1791 when he attended an enthusiastic meeting at the Queen's Head in Norwich. A motion was put and carried that a commission should be obtained under the earlier Act of James I. Under this Act money had been raised to repair the sea breaches between Great Yarmouth and Happisburgh in 1683, 1702 and 1714.

Unfortunately for Berney there was plenty of talk but no real progress, and six months later in January 1792 a single tide overflowed almost a quarter mile inland and several miles wide, again creating havoc when the sea broke through between Waxham and Winterton.[13] It happened again in July. With Waxham Hall once again surrounded by seawater four feet deep he attempted to expedite matters by rallying the other affected landowners. He inserted a notice in the press, reporting that on the evening of 21 July the sea broke through at Waxham and Horsey simultaneously in six places.

He wrote of the 'horrid calamity' he imagined was unfolding hourly in the other affected low-lying areas, and exhorted the landowners to unite in saving the country from being drowned. They should, he wrote, apply immediately to the Seal of England for a Commission to enforce the Act of James I to raise money for the repair of the sea breaches.

His appeal fell on deaf ears once again. The following year another inundation cut off communications between Waxham, Horsey and Winterton, extending three miles inland beyond the village of Hickling, destroying all the fish in the freshwater Hickling Broad. During this single year the dunes between Waxham and Horsey were breached nine times in total, and it took many years for the land to recover its fertility.

As we have seen, Berney's wife and several of his children died between March 1792 and May 1793. The real cause of many diseases was still yet to be discovered. It was believed the rising effluvia which resulted from the repeated flooding 'filled the air with malaria of the worst description' and after the repeated floods of 1792 in particular, 'intermittent and typhoid fevers of a most formidable character prevailed, so that many an individual was brought to a premature grave through this catastrophe.'[14]

Mourning the loss of so many family members in the aftermath of the devastation, and frustrated by the continued inaction, Berney published at his own expense an account of the problems of the sea breaches and what he thought should be done about it. Eventually an Act of Parliament was passed, but still no repair was made. Berney didn't give up. He had a circular printed inviting the Sheriff of Norfolk, Sir John Fenn, to act on the proposed Sea Breach Commission, but Fenn refused. Berney was again devastated by the lack of any real commitment to solve the problem, and Fenn was, as were many others, unsympathetic in the face of his single-minded determination.

While he may have had some economic clout as a major landowner, Berney apparently lacked the necessary administrative influence most often associated with it, and during this period of extreme personal stress his 'singular character' seems to have hampered relations with those he most needed to keep onside. For example, William Windham, later a noted Statesman and orator (at the time M.P for Norwich 1784-1801 with Sir Harbord Harbord), the year before he was made Secretary of War during Pitt's administration, made an entry in his diary for 19 January 1793:

> "Upon coming into the court at Norwich, I was assailed by Sir Berney Brograve, who, in consequence of what had been said by someone respecting them being joined with him in a commission about the sea breaches, wanted to draw from me as he had done from others, a declaration that in similar circumstances no such objection would have been made on my part. Luckily, the singular character of the man put me upon considering the question before I gave an answer; and that consideration showed me that no answer ought to be given at all. The refusal, which greatly astonished him, put him upon talking in a way during dinner which it was necessary to check, but which should have been checked with a lighter hand than that which I found myself using, and which had more an air of quarrelling than I liked to wear, or than the occasion required."[15]

Windham owned an estate at Felbrigg, near Cromer, and had known Berney for many years. They were both early supporters of the Norfolk Militia and he exchanged land with him in 1772 with the Earl of Orford acting as witness. He was also very familiar with the problem of flooding, having already built two windmills to drain several hundred acres of his own marshland. If Berney had been put off by Windham's earlier rebuff and ticking off during dinner, it didn't sway his support for him at the parliamentary elections many years later. It would appear that Windham didn't hold his old acquaintance in the same high regard, however.

National security was the subject on everyone's lips in 1794, and in response to the critical state of Europe Berney attended a meeting at the St Albans Tavern in Norwich. As a life-long supporter of the Norfolk Militia and a contributor to the England Defence Fund, he, together with Lords Walpole, Orford and Townshend, gave one hundred pounds each towards maintaining bodies of cavalry for internal defence.

That year he also wrote to Lord Townshend, then Lord Lieutenant and Vice-Admiral of Norfolk, regarding the preparations to repel Napoleon's threatened invasion. Two of Berney's letters survive, clearly illustrating his unease.

Letters to Marquis Townshend

In the first letter written from Norwich dated 2 May 1794, Berney reminds Townshend that he is a man 'train'd to arms' by his late Royal Highness William Duke of Cumberland and the late General Alexander Drury, and he ventured to inform his Lordship that 'if his Majesty will allow me Arms, Ammunition & Accoutrements I will do all [in] my Power to shew my Attachment to his Majesty, Family and the Government.'

He makes no effort to disguise his nervousness about the situation, warning that the coast between Happisburgh and Yarmouth is vulnerable and defenceless. If in the event the French made good their threat - and it seems no one doubted this eventuality - Berney felt his 'great Property in Corn, Bullocks, & sheep' would be severely endangered. Hoping to elicit a favourable response he offered the incentive: 'I suppose upon an emergency I have sixty Horses of my Own', and adding a sense of urgency he declared himself 'in the greatest Haste, to deliver this information To Coll. Money.'

Colonel Money was a well-known figure in Norwich society. In 1785 the then Major John Money came to the attention of the public in spectacular fashion by ascending in a balloon above the city, but was blown twenty-one miles off course out to sea. A defective valve resulted in the unplanned descent of the balloon and his undignified floundering in the water for four hours till a revenue cutter came to his rescue.

Another slight miscalculation saw him briefly in the service of the French army for six months in 1792. He then abruptly resigned his commission upon hearing of a plan to invade England. When rumours of an invasion became widespread in 1794 Col. Money was at pains to publicly declare his allegiance to England. He dedicated a book on his exploits in France to Marquis Townshend.

Money had inherited a small estate near Norwich and he gave an annual ball which was patronised by leading citizens such as William Windham, and probably also Berney himself. If indeed Berney had been present at Col. Money's ball of 1793 he may have been in Windham's thoughts the next morning, as the latter wrote in his diary - without actually naming names - that he couldn't help but reflect on the 'very low state of talents or understanding in those who compose the whole nearly of the society in Norwich.' More at home in intellectual company such as his friend Dr Johnson, Windham mused: 'The French are surely a more generally enlightened, and polished people.'[16]

Enlightened and polished or not, Berney felt passionately disinclined to welcome the French army onto English soil, but the threat of invasion was only one prong of the trident which relentlessly prodded his diminishing sense of security. The activities of smugglers also continued to cause him anxiety. His discomfort had reached such a low point that he complained to Townshend: 'I feel unpleasant for my personal safety, as I abhor Disloyalty & smuggling. Persons of the last complexion have fired Balls through the sea breaches into my very farm yards'.

Over the years his animosity towards those he believed guilty had rather backfired; the smugglers taunted him and carried on their business regardless. Despite his outward appearance of bluff and bravado Berney had become hostage to his own fear, unable to rest easy at night. It is interesting that he should mention finding cannon balls in his farmyards some fourteen years *after* the London press had first publicised the incident in 1780. This might indicate that either it was common practice for smugglers to lob a few balls in the direction of his house as they passed, or Berney was still fuming nearly a decade and a half later. Whatever the case, the intimidation seems to have had the desired effect.

The second letter to Marquis Townshend, while in the same vein and again written from Norwich, gives further insight into his state of mind. In his first letter, to which he had received Townshend's favourable reply via Colonel Money, he emphasizes his rank as 'Late Captain of Grenadiers in the Norfolk Militia under George Earl of Orford', so he is referring to himself when he makes the point in the second, that 'the services of a respectable officer are always most desirable at this critical period'.

Berney was prepared to 'meet with all due attention, at all events' whatever instructions for coastal defence Marquis Townshend conveyed to him, provided of course that they were 'correspondent to the plans of Government and approved by Parliament'. The marked difference between the two letters in terms of legibility strongly suggests that when Berney started on the second he had already knocked back a good few drinks, having untidily crossed out the very first word he wrote.

Having second thoughts about the position of 'Sir' he had got only as far as the sixth word before it too was crossed out. Thereafter the letter descends into a barely coherent scrawl of what appears to be a drunken jumble of words which overlap each other, half of them added as an afterthought, becoming more condensed as the paper ran out. He has a semi-legible rant about securing the coast against 'Foreign enemies' and outlawing smugglers who 'Fire into the sea breaches at your farms'. This last line and several others he had crossed through as if half-remembering he may have already acquainted Lord Townshend with the despicable act, signing off the whole mess: 'I remain, y^r f^{ll} Servt, Sir Berney Brograve Bart; Norwich'.

He had omitted the date, but judging from the state of his handwriting, by the end of this letter he probably didn't know what day it was anyway. By this time Berney was nearing seventy years of age and was obviously still seething about those cannon balls. After this illuminating missive Lord Townshend may well have wondered at the wisdom of entrusting Berney with anything, let alone the security of Great Britain's vulnerable East Anglia coast in the face of a marauding army.

Happily for Lord Townshend - and more particularly, Berney - France didn't invade England on that occasion, despite William Windham's opposition to all negotiations for peace. But Britain was now in a heightened state of war hysteria aided by the machinations of government, which had been busily grinding away behind the scenes. A plan was hatched to impose a so-called "voluntary loan" on taxpayers to raise money for the war effort, merely a thinly veiled threat of a forced loan if voluntary contributions were not made to the Exchequer.

One bright idea resulted in the Duty on Hair Powder Act which levied a tax on anyone wishing to powder their wig. The practice was already in decline, but from May 1795 all such persons were required to visit a stamp office and purchase an annual certificate for the sum of one guinea. In the seemingly unlikely event that Berney needed to powder his wig, there were several stamp office agents located within a few miles of either of his residences who would willingly oblige him.

The mood of the nation was not soothed by author and politician Edmund Burke, an active contributor to the war hysteria with his writings "Letters on a Regicide Peace". He described the French Revolution and its supporters as a cancer which had to be excised from the body politic. Berney may have agreed but it didn't help him get a better night's sleep.

The constant threat of invasion of his land by seawater only added to his worries. No progress had been made on the question of a Sea Breach Commission by October 1795, when once again Berney's estate suffered 'a most destructive inundation'.[17] The press reported that nearly 1,000 acres of his land were already under water and the sea was making further daily encroachments.

In light of these events the picture becomes clearer as to why Berney gained such a notorious reputation. It was an unfortunate situation that regardless of the causes, the character of such a man did nothing to engender sympathy. Even his brother Thomas found him difficult to deal with. From the early records of the Old Bailey the difference is also evident between Berney's character and that of his apparently agreeable even-tempered father, Thomas senior, well-known in London as a man 'not in the least inclined to be quarrelsome'.

For Berney's detractors - in particular, the working people of his neighbourhood - it wasn't just that they felt oppressed and persecuted. Certainly he was wealthy and belligerent and they were poor and powerless. His behaviour towards them blinded them to the fact that he was pushed almost to his wits end by problems which centred on Waxham. Berney's sanity was relentlessly poked and prodded away at by the repeated inundation of his property, ongoing animosity between himself and the smugglers and the constant fear of foreign invasion. In that last regard his anxieties might have germinated as a young man in the Norfolk Militia when it was embodied in preparation for the threatened invasion in 1759. But while he might have felt more secure in the company of a well-trained army he couldn't change the geography which made his estates so vulnerable.

His frustration was fuelled by reluctance on the part of his peers to ally themselves with his cause – the repairing of the sea breaches in particular. A short temper and self-professed intolerance locked him into a vicious circle, provoking hostility in response. Unable to muster the allegiance of those with influence, Berney instead managed to alienate almost everyone and was left to fight his battles alone. He failed to see that his worst enemy was in fact, himself.

---

[10] The Rural Economy of Norfolk, William Marshall ibid
[11] St James's Chronicle, Nov 7, 1782; Issue 3382
[12] The Rural Economy of Norfolk, William Marshall ibid
[13] General Evening Post (London), Jan 7, 1792; Issue 9093
[14] An Essay On The Encroachments Of The German Ocean Along The Norfolk Coast; William Hewitt, 1844
[15] The Diary of William Windham, 1784 to 1810; edited by H. Baring, 1866 - p. 268
[16] The Diary of William Windham ibid p. 293
[17] Lloyd's Evening Post (London), Oct 14, 1795; Issue 5950

Chapter 5
Two Eventful Years; 1790-92

Acquiring Berney as a father-in-law might have been a daunting prospect for would-be suitors, which might perhaps explain why his two surviving daughters married relatively late. They both lived and found husbands in London, with the eldest, twenty-eight year-old Julian Elizabeth, the first to marry in January 1790. It would be another five years before her sister Anne followed suit, at the age of 32.

Julian's wedding was held at Worstead. Her new husband, Thomas Gregory, formerly of Springfield, Essex, was a prosperous London merchant with his uncle Mark Gregory and brother William. According to their contemporary, Edmund Burke, William was a sometime spy, had been a consul at Mexico, Madrid, Lisbon and Barcelona, and was at times employed on 'confidential missions' by George III in the process of expanding his empire.

1792 was a disastrous year. Barely two years after the marriage, Thomas Gregory's once prosperous life went into a tailspin. His wife Julian somehow survived her hazardous childhood at Waxham only to die two months after their only child Anne was born. The following month Gregory was declared bankrupt and his house and its entire contents were put up for sale to satisfy creditors. Not only the 'excellent and elegant' furniture, but also a harpsichord, 200 ounces of silver plate, paintings, books, clocks, carpets, linen and wine went under the hammer. At the same time, Berney was in the midst of his own disaster. The rest of the family were dying all around him at Waxham after the floods.

After her unfortunate mother's death the infant Anne Gregory was placed under the guardianship of Berney's brother, Thomas Brograve of Springfield Place, and he also made her his heir. Anne led an apparently charmed and privileged life in her great uncle Thomas's household. Two years after his death in 1810 the newly wealthy Anne married Vice Admiral William Beauchamp Proctor of Broome Place, Norfolk, becoming Lady Beauchamp Proctor of Langley Park when her husband succeeded his father as 3rd Baronet in 1827.

A year before the death of his daughter and financial ruin of her husband, Berney nearly came to grief himself. One dark night he was returning to Worstead from Yarmouth in his chaise with his servant when his homeward journey came to a sudden and abrupt halt. The London *Evening Mail* later reported that the horse and chaise, together with its occupants had 'nearly all been precipitated into a deep pit; fortunately their danger was perceived the instant they were on the brink of destruction.' At that moment it would have been most inconvenient for Berney to die a horrible death in the middle of nowhere in the middle of the night. Important plans were afoot. A word or two had been whispered in His Majesty King George's ear; Berney was about to become a baronet.

He had the necessary prerequisites; unswerving commitment to king and country, money and connections. Riding the coattails of his Brograve ancestors would have done him no harm either. The baronetcy had been influenced by his old friend and Colonel of his regiment, George Walpole, 3rd Earl of Orford.[18] From their long association Orford was one of the few who had got to know the real Berney over the years. Formerly Lord of the Bedchamber to George II and afterwards to his son George III, Orford was well-placed to make a recommendation.

On 28 July 1791 Berney became 1st Baronet Brograve of Worstead. In every patent of creation was a clause which entitled the new baronet to have 'a pall supported by two men, a principal mourner and four others' assisting at his funeral. There were other perks, including the right to have the eldest son knighted on his 21st birthday.

The Crown grant, engraved with a portrait of George III and the Royal Arms, acknowledges that Berney freely gave 'aid and supply' to maintain thirty men in the Foot Companies in Ireland 'to continue for three whole years'.[19] Cynics might say Berney merely bought his baronetcy with a contribution to the war chest, a not uncommon practice with obvious benefits for all concerned.

Five months later his friend and ally Lord Orford died of a 'putrid fever' at his seat Houghton Hall in Norfolk, inherited at his father's death forty years earlier when he was 21. In an age of aristocratic excess, Orford had been a genuine eccentric and profligate rake. Unlike Berney, he squandered a good part of his inheritance on horses and greyhounds, but he managed to dig himself out of debt by selling the Houghton collection of paintings, including Van Dykes, Poussins and Rembrandts to Catherine the Great, Empress of Russia, after she offered to take them off his hands for about forty five thousand pounds in 1778. Keen sportsman that he was, it was only natural that he would name a greyhound *Tzarina* to mark the occasion.

After Orford's death his body lay in state at Houghton for several days. The funeral was a grand affair. Chief mourners were Lord Townshend and Orford's uncle and heir Horace Walpole, son of the first Prime Minister Robert Walpole. Specially spruced up for the occasion was the newly-created Sir Berney Brograve, one of eight distinguished pallbearers[20] who conveyed Orford's remains to the family vault at Houghton church. Following closely behind was a procession of one hundred gentlemen and a further one hundred of his tenants. Orford had never married, leaving his uncle Horace to succeed him as fourth Earl.

For Berney, the purchase of a baronetcy didn't come with a bonus set of steak knives and the automatic respect of all his peers. He was still the same man underneath – a man of 'singular character' - as William Windham had noted in his diary just six weeks after Lord Orford's funeral.

---

[18] Chatham Papers: 1783-1806, p.169
[19] Records of Copped Hall Estate, Epping, Ref D/DW/Z2; Essex Record Office
[20] The others were Hon. H. Hobart, Sir J. Woodhouse, Sir Mordaunt Martin, Sir George Chad, Sir Edmund Bacon, Sir Martin Folkes and Sir ThomasBeevor. Star (London, Dec 28, 1791; Issue 1 146.

Chapter 6
The Beginning of the End for Berney

One of Berney's greatest fears - that one day French invaders would land on British soil – did actually occur in his life-time. But only just. On 22 February 1797 a military unit of the French Revolutionary Army (known as *La Legion Noire*) landed 1,200 men, arms and ammunition at Fishguard Bay in Wales with the intention of invading Ireland. Their commander, Colonel William Tate, was a septuagenarian Irish-American veteran of the American Revolutionary conflict.

It was doomed from the start. As soon as a military headquarters was established at Trehavel Farm discipline began to break down amongst many of the irregular soldiers and convicts amongst them. They refused to obey their officers and deserted to loot and pillage nearby villages. A few of the Welsh inhabitants and some French soldiers were killed in the clashes that ensued. The British responded rapidly to the invasion and Colonel Tate was soon in no doubt as to the superior force he was up against. Declining to fight, he surrendered to Lord Cawdor, thus ending the brief two-day French invasion of Britain.

Berney died the day before this inglorious defeat, on 23 February 1797, aged 70, and he was buried seven days later at

Worstead. Coincidentally, Horace Walpole, Earl of Orford, died the same day in London. Walpole was afterwards interred privately at Houghton, and in the absence of any contemporary press report, we can only assume Berney also received a similarly low-key send-off. Berney's last journey on the lonely road from Waxham to Worstead's grand and oversized church would probably have been observed by a few of the local inhabitants who would have felt little sorrow at his passing.

Despite his physical condition, thanks to a penchant for over-indulgence, Berney's relative longevity and survival in the often unhealthy environment in which he raised his family is a testament to the strength of his constitution. This impression of indestructibility may have discomforted the long-suffering locals after so many years subjected to the idiosyncrasies of his character. For them his death may have been rather a relief. Any semblance of a ripe old age eluded Berney's children however, and all but three of his sons died before their majority. Having made no will his estate was administered soon after his death, his son George succeeding to his properties and title.

This brings us to the throat-cutting legend in the attic of Waxham Hall. It's an unlikely story. As the burial records show, the Brograves didn't do anything by halves when it came to deaths in the family. Just eight weeks before Berney died the London press had reported the news that yet another of his sons, twenty-year-old John, had died at Waxham. The family would still have been at high risk of malaria, given the recent invasive flooding of the land surrounding the Hall. Perhaps Berney and his son had both contracted the disease.

A grisly death by suicide would not have escaped the attention of the press, ever eager to titillate their readers. John had been taking the waters at Bath during his illness and *The Bath Chronicle* later reported that he had died of 'a consumption'. Announcing Berney's demise, *The Gentleman's Magazine* makes no mention of anything untoward, paling the attic story to an imaginative but improbable yarn.

Certainly Berney kept himself in a heightened state of anxiety over England's conflict with the French. Fuelled by an alarmist government, the information filtered through his militia contacts saw to that. But despite his long-held fears the timing of the invasion is an unconvincing catalyst for suicide. A fighter to his last breath, he would never have done something so unpatriotic.

Besides, he would hardly have known of their unwelcome and much dreaded arrival, since three French frigates had only first been spotted the day before his death off Ilfracombe in Devon, on the opposite side of the country. News could travel only as fast as a horse could run. By the time it reached Norwich more than 300 miles away the last vestige of life had already left Berney's bloated body. Whatever the true cause of Berney's death, there was a reasonable chance he had already pickled his liver.

Berney had been gone barely a month when word got around that some of his property was to be put up for sale. During his lifetime he had mortgaged his estates, probably in part to build Worstead House. He had been careful with his expenditure for a reason. George, his heir, now lumbered with his father's debt, decided to divest himself of the smaller properties.

The availability of one of these properties came to the notice of a well-known Norfolk man, the newly promoted Admiral, Horatio Nelson. He was a cousin of Berney's second wife and also a relative of the Walpoles. Nelson had not long finished fighting the Battle of Cape St. Vincent in February 1797 when his wife Fanny wrote from Bath that she had heard of a house in the constituency which might suit them. She was aware of her husband's political aspirations after Henry Jodrell won the seat of Great Yarmouth in the parliamentary elections of October 1796.

There had been much dissatisfaction with their new MP-elect; the voters really wanted a naval man to represent them. The celebrated Admiral would fit the bill nicely. Nelson's wife told him: 'Mr. Lucas mentioned a house and twenty acres of land that would soon be offered for sale eight miles from Norwich either in the Bury or Bungay road; which - I am not certain. The house is not large, two very good parlours and a study, the house was Sir Barney Bargraves'.[21]

Nelson was given command of *HMS Theseus* after the battle of Cape St. Vincent and was neither able nor inclined to head home on hearing this news. Had he done so he might not have lost his right arm three months later during an unsuccessful attack on Santa Cruz, Tenerife. Only then did a homeward journey suddenly become a priority, and naturally right handed, Nelson wrote soon afterwards in shaky left handed script to Admiral Sir John Jervis: 'I hope you will be able to give me a frigate to convey the remains of my carcase to England …. the sooner I get to a very humble cottage the better.'[22] But the Nelsons didn't buy Sir Berney's little house.

---

[21] Nelson's Letters To His Wife: and Other Documents, 1785-1831; Frances Nelson 1958
[22] The Dispatches and Letters of Vice Admiral Lord Viscount Nelson, Vol. 2; Sir Nicholas Harris Nicolas, 1845

Chapter 7
A Family in Decline

Berney's grandfather Thomas Brograve Snr knew he was dying when he wrote his will in 1691. He also knew his wife was pregnant. She gave birth to their son Thomas Jnr (Berney's father) soon after the burial of her husband at Brisley, a tiny village 36 miles east of Waxham. Under the terms of his father's will, young Thomas was to receive a legacy of five hundred pounds. All property went to his eldest brother Edward with other cash legacies to the younger children.

It was expected that Thomas would have to earn his own living, and when he was seventeen his father's executors arranged an apprenticeship with Peter Chesshyre of the Tallow Chandlers Company in London, following in the footsteps of his brother Augustine. But soon Augustine died, and their brother Edward, as well as both sisters, Rebecca and Elizabeth.

By outliving all four of his siblings Berney's father landed himself an unexpected windfall. At his majority he came into possession of his father's estates in male entail, and he was also heir-at-law to his spendthrift cousin Sir Thomas Brograve, 3rd baronet of Hamels. Although elevated to the status of landowner and gentleman he was in no rush to find a wife. By the time he married in July 1725 he was thirty-three.

Financially secure with property and rental income, he made his home base at his father's former property at Althorne in Essex, less than 50 miles north-east of London. Elite society in the 18th century considered London the capital of the world, so too did Thomas who spent much of his time in the city. There he married Berney's mother, Miss Julian Berney. Her parents were John Berney of Westwick, Norfolk, and his wife Bridget Branthwaite.

A wealthy landed family, the Berneys were also the subject of macabre folklore. Julian's great-grandfather Sir Richard Berney was created 1st Baronet of Parkhall in the reign of James I, and his coat of arms bore the Red Hand of Ulster, the badge of baronetcy. The legend grew that the Berneys were forced to wear a 'bloody hand' in their arms as a punishment after one of the family had long ago 'whipped a boy to dead'.[23] Perhaps there is a grain of truth in the story: Sir Richard apparently had an unforgiving temperament. He disinherited his eldest son Thomas, leaving his estate of Reedham to his younger son Richard. In doing so he merely postponed the disintegration of his estate until the next generation. His grandson dissipated his fortune and sold Reedham, thus mirroring the fate of the Brograves of Hamels. *See Chapter XI; Extinction of a Dynasty.*

As the eldest son of a younger son, Julian's father John Berney inherited the manor of Westwick, originally purchased by Sir Richard Berney, who would probably have considered this grandson a more worthy successor. John fared considerably better than his profligate cousin Thomas Berney. His improved status is illustrated by the names of his pallbearers in 1730 - amongst which were Lords Hobart and Walpole, when he was 'handsomely interr'd' at Westwick.[24]

Having no sons, John Berney left his real estate to the male heirs of his younger daughter Elizabeth. To his eldest daughter Mrs. Julian Brograve he left his personal estate. According to local tradition, Elizabeth's husband William Petre had an obelisk built at the edge of Westwick Park after she fell out with her sister Julian, living less than a mile away at Worstead. The idea was that she and her husband could spy on the Brograves. The 90 foot high obelisk survives but is now derelict and the iron-roofed observatory at the top is gone. This noted landmark features on the Westwick village sign.

Julian Berney's marriage with Thomas Brograve added to an already convoluted tangle of interconnections: his mother Susannah Jessop's first two husbands were both Brograves. At her marriage to Thomas's father, Susannah was the widow of the latter's uncle, Augustine Brograve, with whom she had a daughter Jemima. Jemima married William Branthwaite of the Middle Temple, Julian's uncle and father of the man Thomas killed in the duel in London in 1726.

Berney's Siblings
The Lawyer; Thomas Brograve

A year or so younger than Berney, seventeen year-old Thomas was apprenticed to Robert Moxon, attorney of Bernards Inn, London, one of the eight Inns of Chancery. It would prove to be an enduring association lasting more than four decades. Two hundred and ten pounds of his father's money secured the apprenticeship in 1744 and he was admitted to the Inner Temple the following year. At his father's death eight years later he inherited several properties in Suffolk and Norfolk, providing a welcome boost to his income. Messrs Moxon and Brograve were a partnership by 1766, and in his will Moxon later appointed him as one of the trustees of his estate.

When Moxon retired aged nearly eighty Thomas took over the business. In a deal 'too lucky a circumstance to be refused',[25] Thomas was said to be selling his practice to Thomas Blake of Norwich, and one of Moxon's nephews. It was reported in 1779 that Mr Brograve laid down 'hard terms, but they say they must be complyed with'. Thomas eventually set up another law practice in partnership with William Lyon at Coney Court, Gray's Inn, which continued until at least 1783.

Two years earlier he had purchased an estate in Chelmsford called Springfield Place, perhaps with a view to his retirement from London life. The 18th century house is built of red brick with two storeys, a dormer windowed attic and an outlook onto the verdant expanse of Springfield Green directly opposite. In the grounds is also a very large two storey coach house. The house, elegant and commodious, was a moderately spectacular measure of Thomas's success. But he had not purchased it to quarter a tribe of offspring; by then he was fifty-four years-old and a confirmed bachelor. Rather he rattled around in it with only his younger unmarried sister Anne and their young niece Anne Gregory - who were greatly outnumbered by a team of bustling servants.

Apparently Thomas did not share Berney's quirky personality traits, nor unsurprisingly, did they always see eye to eye. For the sake of his own good reputation and sanity he probably kept contact between them to a minimum. As for their mother Julian, she continued to live with her seven servants at Great Baddow after their father's death. She may have seen less of Berney than her other children because he lived further away. As she lay on her deathbed towards the end of 1767 a certain Mr Griffenhoofe came to bleed her (for which he charged five shillings) and a doctor by the name of Pugh attended her morning and evening. She died in late November without making a will. Thomas was appointed administrator of her estate, and inevitably a dispute arose between the two brothers over her possessions.

Berney wasted no time in travelling to his mother's house to secure his entitlement. Thomas, then living in London, was unaware of Berney's trip to Baddow until after the event. He discovered that Berney, in cahoots with his other siblings, had made an inventory and appraisal of Julian's goods in his absence. They had grossly overvalued everything - he believed - and as if to prove his point he had offered the goods several times to Berney to purchase at the appraised value. Each time he refused them. Thomas then made his own inventory and a more realistic valuation (totalling less than £630), which did not include his mother's clothing or other personal items. He insisted everything his mother left belonged only to himself, his brother William and sister Anne as residuary legatees. Berney disagreed and took Thomas to court.

With thinly disguised antagonism Thomas made a written declaration that Berney, 'the person promoting this cause', could have no demands on any share or distribution of their mother's personal estate because its value fell short of the expenses, including his bill for administration. He made the point that at their father's death fourteen years earlier their mother was to have all his plate, linen, household goods, pictures, coach and a pair of horses with accoutrements. After her death these were to go to Berney.

But as sole executrix she had made no inventory or appraisal of her late husband's goods and later 'exchanged away or disposed of' some of the items. Thomas said his mother was in the habit of 'often declaring that what she should buy and leave on the premises at her death should go to her younger children in lieu thereof'. In retrospect, he was somewhat critical of his mother's actions in keeping possession of much of the contents of the house and farm without ever accounting for any of it to her younger children.

She had lived a comfortable widow's life with her household servants and caged parrot. The servants tended three bee hives, raised a number of pigs, cattle and chickens. Compiling his own inventory Thomas counted nearly one hundred items in his mother's large collection of blue and white china, and she apparently had a particular penchant for green checked upholstery. Sofas, chairs and mattresses were all covered in it, with an extra ten yards in reserve. Bed sheets (31) were slightly less abundant than tablecloths (47) and amongst other things, her pantry included 36 pots of jelly and 65 gallipots of raspberry jam. There was also a well-stocked cellar including wine, brandy, whiskey, rum and cider. There were close to one hundred bottles in total, and not all of it paid for - as Thomas later discovered.

Unbeknown to Thomas and before he was ready to distribute her personal effects, Berney had instigated the division and separation of their mother's effects into five lots; one for their niece and the other four between them. Thomas was annoyed and complained he saw nothing of the lot drawn for him in his absence except for two or three common gold mourning rings. We can only imagine how this little saga ended, but it would be reasonable to assume that it wasn't resolved by inviting Berney for a friendly cup of tea and a brotherly chat.

Unlike Berney, whose disposition tended to alienate rather than cultivate friends, Thomas enjoyed the respect of his peers, holding an appointment as a Governor of Magdalen Hospital between 1790 and 1798. He was on the Commission of the Peace and appointed Deputy Lieutenant of Essex in 1797. In his various roles as executor and trustee of several deceased estates and guardian to his niece Anne Gregory, Thomas either instigated or was involved in a number of lawsuits over the years, but only one with Berney. He died at Springfield Place in December 1810 at the unusually old age (for a Brograve) of 83, a wealthy bachelor, 'universally beloved and respected'. His remains were interred in a vault under the family pew in the church of Allsaints, Springfield.

The Naval Officer; Captain William Brograve

Their youngest brother William (b. circa 1729), joined the Royal Navy when he was about sixteen. After serving two terms of three years each as midshipman, the second of these under the command of Captain George Brydges Rodney (later Vice Admiral), William was anxious to advance his career. In May 1752 William's father Thomas wrote to Secretary of State Lord Holderness asking if he would put in a good word on William's behalf to the Admiral of the Fleet, Lord Anson. William, who had his sights set on a promotion as acting Lieutenant, was keen to join Captain Cockburn who was readying his ship to sail for the Guinea Station.

Thomas optimistically suggested to Lord Holderness that if his request was granted, and if any officers happened to die during the voyage, William might be nominated to succeed them. Confirmation of William's suitability would be obtained on request from his previous two commanders, Thomas confidently assured him. They would 'certify that he behaved well, with diligence and great sobriety', and he promised to give William an allowance 'consistent with that rank and station'.

The request found favour in all the right quarters and William was officially promoted to Lieutenant in August 1753. He received an assurance from Lord Holderness that if he behaved himself well and he (Lord H.) received favourable reports of his continuing good character, William could expect further patronage and advancement. Four months later William's father died, leaving him two hundred pounds and property in Norfolk at Shipdham and Bradenham.

Meanwhile trouble was brewing abroad, and unlike his brother Berney, who involved himself in homeland defence with the Norfolk militia, for the next few years William lived an adventurous shipboard life. In 1756 the Prime Minister, the Duke of Newcastle, was optimistic that a new set of alliances would prevent the outbreak of war in Europe. However the French, who had been menacing the

British garrison on the island of Minorca in the Mediterranean, launched a pre-emptive strike. Thus began the Seven Years War (1756-1763) and William soon found himself right in the thick of it.

At the beginning of hostilities an attempt to save Minorca was foiled during a sea battle involving a squadron of ten British ships under the command of Admiral John Byng. The overseer of naval operations, Lord Anson, had been particularly concerned at the prospect of a threatened invasion of Britain by the French, and kept in reserve some of the fleet to protect their home territory. Consequently he was criticised after the fall of Minorca for not sending enough ships with Admiral Byng. He briefly left the Admiralty, but it was Byng who paid the ultimate price for the failure.

Initially the British public was outraged by the defeat and in January 1757 Byng was brought home to be tried by court-martial for breach of the Articles of War. This had recently undergone amendment to mandate capital punishment for all officers who failed to do their utmost against the enemy, either in battle or pursuit (rather than the previously discriminatory rule that only lesser-ranking officers were subject to the death penalty).

Byng was acquitted of personal cowardice and disaffection, and convicted only for not having done his utmost, since he failed to pursue the superior French fleet to protect his own. Despite the lesser conviction, the court had no discretion under the Articles of War to impose a more fitting punishment, and Byng was sentenced to death. A request for a royal prerogative of mercy was presented by the new First Lord of the Admiralty, Lord Temple, but after an unsatisfactory exchange with King George the request was denied.

Byng's fate was sealed. He was taken under guard to be confined on *HMS Monarque* in Portsmouth Harbour to await execution.

While all this was going on Lieutenant William Brograve was enthusiastically recruiting for the war effort. A year earlier, just prior to the Battle of Minorca, he was employed on shore at Great Yarmouth, and spent the next seven months "recruiting" reluctant seamen for His Majesty's service 'with good success and ease to the inhabitants'. Lord Holderness was acquainted with this pleasing intelligence by William himself, and at the same time he requested to be assigned to a sloop. The legality or otherwise of coercing men into naval service was a question that has never been satisfactorily explained. On the impress system of the eighteenth century, John Hutchinson puts into graphic perspective William's allusion to its ready acceptance by the people, in his book *The Press-Gang Afloat and Ashore* (1913):

> "In its inception, its development, and more especially in its extraordinary culmination, it perhaps constitutes the greatest anomaly, as it undoubtedly constitutes the grossest imposition, any free people ever submitted to. Although unlawful in the sense of having no foundation in law, and oppressive and unjust in that it yearly enslaved, under the most noxious conditions, thousands against their will, it was nevertheless for more than a hundred years tolerated and fostered as the readiest, speediest and most effective means humanly devisable for the manning of a fleet whose toll upon a free people, in

the same period of time, swelled to more than thrice its original bulk.

Standing as a bulwark against aggression and conquest, it ground under its heel the very people it protected, and made them slaves in order to keep them free. Masquerading as a protector, it dragged the wage-earner from his home and cast his starving family upon the doubtful mercies of the parish. And as if this were not enough, whilst justifying its existence on the score of public benefit it played havoc with the fisheries, clipped the wings of the merchant service, and sucked the life-blood out of trade."

None of these sobering consequences would have occurred to, or probably even concerned William, who was merely an ambitious young officer following orders for the better defence of England against the French. In May 1756 his old commander Captain Rodney had taken command of the *Monarque* at Plymouth, a 74 gun 'ship of the line', - a three-masted square-rigged vessel - which had some years earlier been captured from the French during the Battle of Cape Finisterre. Captain Rodney began to fit and man the ship for service. He assigned William as Lieutenant in January 1757 under the command of Captain John Montagu, and William was one of the officers into whose custody, one month later, the unfortunate but defiant Admiral Byng was secured.

Byng's date of execution was set for 28 February, but at the last minute a fourteen day respite was granted by the king. When the new warrant for execution arrived at Portsmouth with a warning by the Admiralty to take extra care their prisoner did not escape, Byng's previous routine of confinement was tightened. Captain Montagu noted in his log: "Received orders to put a stronger guard on Mr. Byng". Admiral Edward Boscawen, who had signed the death warrant, ordered that one of the ship's officers be with Byng at all times, night and day.

Captain Montagu selected Lieutenants Brograve, Shirley, Uvedale and Lambert for the task, relieving each other every four hours. Each was required to keep a written record of their watch, and at the beginning of his four hour shifts William entered the details of the change of the guard in the log-book. He then settled down for his vigil with Byng in the captain's cabin, where a light was kept burning all night. During the day the names of all Byng's visitors were noted in a journal, what time they arrived, and again before dark when they left.

After a day and night of gale-force wind which buffeted all the ships in Portsmouth Harbour, the morning of 14 March 1757 dawned with comparative calm. A small area of the quarterdeck of the *Monarque* was strategically sprinkled with sawdust, and at midday William witnessed Byng's controversial execution by firing squad, an event since viewed as a low point in British Naval history.

The following month the *Monarque* set sail from Spithead to St Helen's to await the first wind for the Mediterranean. A British squadron was attempting to capture the French fortress of Louisbourg on Île Royale (now known as Cape Breton Island). The *Monarque* had orders to join Henry Osborn's fleet to intercept a French squadron attempting to relieve pressure on the rest of the Toulon fleet at Louisbourg. In October, while the *Monarque* was anchored at the British base in Gibraltar Bay just south of Carthagena Bay (where they not long afterwards blockaded the French squadron), William was feeling restless and frustrated that he still had not been commissioned to command a sloop - which was promised ten months earlier. He again wrote to Lord Holderness: 'My Lord Temple promised Mr. Geo. Townshend that he would appoint me to the command of a sloop as there has been thirty junior Lieutenants that have got the command of sloops and some to Post ships. I am fearful I am forgot'.

For whatever reason, William's ambition was kept in limbo for almost another three years until 1760, when he came to the attention once again of Captain Rodney, busily organising ships and men for duty in the English Channel. Rodney had received orders from the Admiralty in September for the *Albany*, *Bonetta*, and *Roast Beef* to provide protection to the island of Jersey by cruising the Channel, but William, the newly appointed commander of the 16-gun sloop *Albany* was proving elusive. Complaining that 'no officer [had] appeared with their orders to command the Albany', Rodney ordered Lieutenant William Bensley of the *Deptford* to command her, 'till their Lordships' pleasure be known, she has been sailed several days to her station.' William's failure to appear was disrupting Rodney's plans, and two weeks later the Admiralty was again advised that Lieutenant Brograve had still not made his appearance.

William did eventually present himself for duty, and he was promoted to Captain with a crew of 125 men under his command. His exploits capturing French privateer vessels running the gauntlet in the English Channel received publicity in the press during 1761. In March he took the privateer *Hazard* off the Isle of Wight, apparently without a fight. In April it was reported that he fell in with the French Frigate *Pheasant* off Plymouth during daylight, chasing her all night till ten the next morning.

The *Albany* drew alongside and William gave the order to open fire. The *Pheasant* hoisted the French flag and retaliated with guns blazing. Or at least, what remained of her guns. When the chase began, the French vessel had equal fire-power with the *Albany*, but her Captain, M. La Courdray had ordered fourteen of their guns to be thrown overboard - leaving only two, thus making them no match for William and his crew. They brought their prize triumphantly into Spithead, near Portsmouth.

One observer later remarked that the inequality of sixteen guns against two made it appear a cheap victory. The fact that the *Pheasant* was 24 feet longer than the Albany promoted the more patriotic view that its capture by Captain Brograve reflected honour on the nation and on the officers and men. Particularly when the enemy had so feared engaging with an inferior force it threw most of its guns overboard in hope of escaping by an ignominious flight. Two days later they captured a French frigate, the *Tourterelle* off Guernsey, and over the course of the next few weeks another three French coasting vessels surrendered to their control. Each of these successes was rewarded by bounty money and a share from the profits of confiscated cargo, and the prizes were beginning to mount.

At the same time, the Navy, under the command of Admiral Augustus Keppel, was smarting from defeat after a failed attempt to capture the French Belle Île in April 1761, but a second successful attempt was made with reinforcements a few weeks later when they besieged the island. William was sent in the *Albany* to replenish supplies to the British fleet occupying the defenceless ports. He returned to Portsmouth in June after the French commander agreed to capitulate. For the remainder of 1761 William resumed his cruise duty of the Channel, which was for the most part uneventful - with the exception of an incident in November when the *Albany* limped back to port minus her topmasts after a severe storm.

When Spain reluctantly entered hostilities against England on the side of France and Austria, Britain seized the opportunity to capture the Cuban city of Havana. Plans were underway in February 1762 for an amphibious attack by an expedition under the command of Admiral George Keppel (brother of Augustus) with Vice-Admiral Sir George Pocock as naval commander. Utilising one of his brother Berney's connections, William wrote in February to the Hon. George Townshend M.P., (later Lord Townshend) asking that he use his influence so he could sail in the *Albany* or a larger ship under the orders of Vice-Admiral Pocock to accompany the British fleet. It appears he may have indeed got his wish for a larger ship; a Captain Thomas Symonds was given the *Albany* in his place two weeks later.

As far as the battle for Havana is concerned, the British emerged victorious in August despite a valiant fight put up by the Spaniards. A year later England gave Havana back to Spain along with Manila as part of the Treaty of Paris that ended the Seven Years' War. William by this time was not much more than thirty and had packed a lot into his years as a loyal young naval officer, but while Uvedale, his fellow Lieutenant on board the *Monarque* was later promoted to Admiral, William never advanced beyond the rank of Captain. After the hostilities ended in 1763 the records fall silent on Captain William Brograve. He probably resigned from the Navy and retired to Shipdham to farm his land, where he appears in 1768 on a Poll to elect a Knight of the Shire for Norfolk.

He appointed his brother Thomas executor of his estate, and after his death in 1784 his farm stock at Shipdham, implements of animal husbandry, brewing utensils and household furniture were put up for auction. William had never married, but from information contained in his will it is probable that he fathered six children, although he doesn't specifically claim them as his own. Firstly he names Thomas, Mary, Henry and George - whom he describes as 'natural children of Rebecca Ironson deceased', his former housekeeper, who were born just after the end of the Seven Years War between 1764 and 1774 - according to the Shipdham parish register.

The surname is recorded as Ireson, and no father named. Their mother died in 1776. William engaged a new housekeeper, Frances Cliffen, who also gave birth to two illegitimate children, Edward and Frances, born in 1782 and 1783, both named in William's will. This in itself may not necessarily be significant; perhaps they all lived under his roof and he had simply developed a fondness for them, but perhaps there was more to their mothers' job description than merely 'keeping house'. Having two successive housekeepers with several illegitimate children between them is rather too coincidental to dismiss.

To each of these children he bequeathed 150 pounds, a significant sum which collectively would amount to somewhere between fifty and sixty thousand pounds today. This generosity is all the more remarkable since despite having ten nephews and nieces living, none rated a mention, except the unnamed youngest son of his brother Berney, to whom he left his entailed real estate. (Berney's son, Sir George Berney Brograve, outlived all his brothers, so this property devolved on to him).

The children of William's household were more fortunate than most of the many spurious progeny recorded in the county parish registers. About a century later *The National Review*,[26] the platform of the British Conservative Party, asserted that population statistics in Norfolk showed 'the number of idiots is considerably larger than in any other equal district of England, and the illegitimate births are more numerous'. The reason for this was apparently that 'the dwellers in East Anglia are not a very high order of humanity' - presumably compared to those who characterised the more elite society of London, for example, and in particular, Conservative Party members and their supporters.

Two years after William's death, parish records indicate his housekeeper, Frances Cliffen, had another illegitimate child to a certain Robert Butcher. In 1788, respecting his brother's wishes, Thomas Brograve, his executor, paid for the apprenticeship of at least one of the Ironson boys, George, to a shoemaker in Shipdham.

The Plantation Owner's Wife; Elizabeth Brograve

The marriage settlement between twenty-one year-old Elizabeth , the eldest of Berney's sisters, and her new husband, William Matthew of Great Baddow, involved West Indian plantations, slaves, sugar and rum works, with a conjunction of properties in Tillingham, Dengie and High Hall, Walthamstow, all in Essex. The latter had been inherited by Elizabeth from her father Thomas Brograve, and the former by William from his grandfather Sir William Matthew, Governor of the Leeward Islands, a British colony comprising chiefly of Antigua, St. Kitts and Nevis, Anguilla and Montserrat.

Subsequent to Elizabeth and William's marriage in London in May 1754, they had a daughter, Julian Catherine, but both parents had died by the time their child was aged about ten, leaving her an orphan. While she was still a minor, Julian's guardians, her uncle Thomas and his sister Anne Brograve, along with two other family members, gave their consent to her marriage in 1773 to John Conyers the younger, heir to Copt Hall, Essex. Julian - known as Julia - as great-niece to Sir Berney Brograve would unwittingly provide a future inheritor of his estates. It would have been inconceivable at that time - not least to Berney - that her son Henry John Conyers (b. 1782) would one day inherit his estates as the controversial and unpopular heir-at-law to Berney's son George.

Julia Matthew had inherited her father's plantations on two West Indian islands in 1764, and as a consequence of her marriage John Conyers came into possession in right of his wife. As an absentee proprietor, Conyers had the plantations under management, and when the French Admiral de Grasse, as part of a general conquest of the West Indies, landed a strong force on St. Kitts in February 1782, Conyers suffered losses of crops during the siege.

His Negroes absconded and the French established a camp on one of his plantations, which, to his annoyance, met with no counter-action by the British troops then on the nearby southern island of St. Lucia. Conyers was advised to either sell the Negroes on his plantation in Antigua or move them to St. Kitts, but he came up against resistance from Berney's brother Thomas Brograve. Thomas wrote to him in 1783 advising that the removal of Negroes to St. Kitts would be a breach of the marriage settlement.

Julia seems to have held a special place in her uncle's affections and he generously left her four thousand pounds at his death.

The Prim Spinster; Anne Brograve

Berney's youngest sister Anne was sixteen when their father died. She inherited his property in Essex at Althorne, as well as land in Norfolk at Waxham and Ryeborough. Choosing not to live with her widowed mother, initially she lived at Bexfield, not far from Great Baddow with her brother Thomas, afterwards moving in with him later when he purchased Springfield Place.

Their co-habitation was apparently a happy arrangement, further demonstrating the contrast between Berney and his siblings. Anne later requested her burial in the vault in Springfield church near the remains of her brother, and 'that as we have lived in perfect unity together, so may together have a part in the resurrection of the just.' She had never married. Instead she filled the role of substitute mother and grandmother to her niece Julia Matthew and great-niece Anne Gregory, both raised by Anne and Thomas.

Anne Brograve's will, dated 5 July 1819,[27] demonstrates her affection for Anne Gregory, and she was also very generous towards her other nephews and nieces. But in stark contrast to her brother Thomas she had a fractious relationship with her eldest niece Julia Matthew, by then Mrs John Conyers. Initially, in what appears to be a token bequest, Anne had left Julia a mere fifty pounds and an annuity of the same amount. By comparison she left two thousand pounds to Berney's son George and one thousand each to several other nephews and nieces, as well as great-nephews and nieces - including eleven hundred pounds to Julia's son Henry.

Perhaps 82 year-old Aunt Anne had already intimated this expression of her disaffection to Julia; just nine days after writing her will they had a furious row which was never resolved. Eight months later Anne instructed her solicitor to add what became a lengthy three page codicil to include many more beneficiaries, and apparently in a fit of pique she revoked all legacies to Julia 'in consequence of ill treatment and behaviour towards me on the 14th July last'. Thus Julia was completely banished from her affections. Anne was still sharp as a tack; age had dimmed neither her memory nor her feistiness. She died three months later in May 1820 and was buried according to her wishes, in the vault with her brother at Springfield church.

Anne's 'dear niece' Anne Gregory, wife of Captain William Beauchamp Proctor, was by this time the mother of four children. Her aunt had requested Anne and William 'sit for the most eminent artist' to have their portraits painted. The same artist was to reproduce a larger portrait of her brother Thomas from a miniature - which she had always considered a good likeness and well executed.

Anne left her niece all her real estate and household effects, and made a point of reminding her that 'Her obligations to her uncle from the time of her birth, are so great that they cannot be too much encumbered by her desire that the whole of the expense of those three pictures may be defrayed out of my funded property. I would have no expense spared to have them well done and handsomely framed'.

In remembrance of the mother she never knew, and also out of respect for her guardians, Anne's niece named her eldest son Thomas William Brograve Beauchamp Proctor when he was born in 1815. He succeeded his father as 4th Baronet in 1861, two years after his mother's death. He later reversed the order of the names to take the style of Proctor Beauchamp in place of Beauchamp Proctor.

The name of Brograve reappeared in 1897 in the person of Sir Brograve Campbell Beauchamp, Anne Gregory's great grandson, who succeeded his father Sir Edward as 2nd Baronet of Grosvenor Place, Westminster in 1925. Apart from being M.P for Walthamstowe between 1931 and 1945, Sir Brograve's other claim to fame is as the son-in-law of the 5th Earl of Carnarvon of Highclere Castle (Downton Abbey of television fame), the celebrated excavator of Tutankhamen's tomb. Sir Brograve's wife Lady Evelyn Herbert was with her father when the tomb was discovered at Luxor.

---

[23] The Lore of the Land, ibid
[24] Daily Post (London), 2 October 1730; Issue 3444
[25] Norfolk Record Society: Vol 67, 1931
[26] Ibid Vol.19, 1892
[27] Prob 11/1633

Chapter 8
The Survivors

Sir George Berney Brograve, 2nd Baronet

Destined to outlive all but one of his sixteen siblings, George, born and baptised at Worstead, was Berney's third child and first son with his second wife. Although he managed to avoid the animosity that had shadowed his father, he was still in for a rough ride. Berney had been dead about nine years when George's marital misfortunes were plastered all over the British press.

Unlike his father, George appears to have endeared himself somewhat to the disaffected poor of Worstead. In April 1799 he gave a fat bullock and 500 three-penny loaves to be distributed amongst them, and on Christmas Day 1801 he 'gave 430 poor persons in Worstead a plentiful dinner of beef and bread, which proved a great relief'. He also provided ten pounds a year for ten children to be taught school at Palling.

No doubt at his father's urging - and ever mindful of the need to protect British soil from the invading French - George had gained a commission as Captain in the Western Regiment of the Norfolk Militia late in 1794. He served under the command of Col. Hon. Horatio Walpole, and during the course of the next four years he rose up the ranks. By the time he resigned in June 1799 he had succeeded to the baronetcy and was owner of his late father's estates.

On the war front, tensions between England and France appeared less threatening than they had been during the latter part of his father's life. George had done his duty and could at last relax and enjoy his gentleman's life at Worstead. Twenty miles to the southeast in Yarmouth, the mood was still buoyant a year later when the town feted the returning hero Horatio Nelson, accompanied by his mistress Lady Hamilton. Not long afterwards the sky over Norwich lit up with fireworks celebrating the ratification of peace between England and France. A good time to get married, George must have thought. And so he did. His bride was Miss Emma Louisa Whitwell, earmarked to inherit half her father's estates.

Everyone, including George, had been lulled into a false sense of security about the French situation, but before long elation would be replaced by old anxieties once again. Emboldened by recent victories in Europe, Napoleon was still hostile towards England and continued his grandiose and elaborate plans of conquest. Prompted by renewed belligerence from across the Channel, George rejoined the Eastern Regiment in November 1802, an appointment which would prove detrimental to his marriage.

A few months later the Secretary of War, William Windham, warned parliament that Bonaparte was 'the Hannibal who has sworn to devote his life to the destruction of England. War cannot be far off and I believe that it would be much safer to anticipate the blow than to expect it'. The government was in a state of financial collapse from previous war expenditure and loss of Continental markets. Britain couldn't afford a war just yet. In January 1803 Prime Minister Addington made a public declaration: Britain was in a profound state of peace. It was brief. With finances sufficiently recovered, war was finally declared against France in May, ending the uneasy truce created by the Treaty of Amiens.

In June George's regiment was embodied at its depot in Norfolk before marching to Colchester. It was here that his marriage had first begun to unravel. George accompanied his regiment when it moved to the south coast, serving first at Winchelsea and then, in the following year, at Hastings. He was raised to the rank of Lieutenant Colonel in 1805. In February 1806 his regiment returned to the Eastern Region, firstly to Chelmsford, then back to Colchester.

By this time his marital situation was seriously compromised. He resigned a few weeks later in May 1806, just as Britain enacted a naval blockade of the French coasts. In response Napoleon created his own blockade. He issued the Berlin Decree designed to stifle the British economy and create civil unrest. For George, the manoeuvrings of the French were the last thing he wanted to think about right at that moment; his mind was on problems closer to home.

A frequent visitor to Bath, he had met his future wife there in 1797, the year of his father's death. His younger brother John was also very ill and he had accompanied him to take the waters. By chance he met Emma's father, Edward Whitwell, 'a Gentleman of fortune and consequence' and a former envoy to the Court at

Versailles during the French Revolution. George – excellent son-in-law material as far as Whitwell was concerned – was introduced to his two daughters. Over the course of the next two years he became smitten with Emma, the youngest of the two.

But the feeling was not altogether mutual and Emma would later complain that he had made his proposal of marriage firstly to her father, who had given his consent without her knowledge or approval. Twenty-eight year-old George and his reluctant eighteen year-old bride were married at Bath in May 1800. The new Lady Brograve came with a fortune described variously as between ten thousand and seventeen thousand pounds, and she was provided with an annual allowance of one thousand pounds in accordance with their marriage settlement.

They had barely settled in at Worstead House when a fire broke out, threatening destruction of the whole building. Due to the quick actions of George and some of his servants it was confined to just one room, leaving him with a repair bill of two hundred pounds. Three weeks later during a fierce storm he proved himself a selfless hero when two large colliers were wrecked at Palling and Waxham. Eight men lost their lives but the rest were saved 'due in great degree' to his exertions.

He had just been nominated Sheriff of Norfolk and was subsequently nominated several more times, although he was never actually elected. In company with other eminent citizens he served on the Grand Jury at the Norwich Assizes, assisting in the dispatch of criminals either to their death for petty crimes such as stealing a horse or a couple of sheep, or if they were lucky, banishment to a penal colony in Australia.

Lady Brograve's 'Criminal Conversation'

In July 1807 George sat in the Court of the King's Bench with a heavy heart. He had brought a charge of Criminal Conversation against Captain Marsham Elwin, the dastardly young libertine accused of seducing and debauching his wife. In his preamble, the Attorney General, who acted on George's behalf, said that Sir George was a former lawyer, but being possessed of a great fortune had retired from public practice at his father's death, taking up residence at Worstead House. The first few years of George and Emma's married life were spent happily in 'a retired situation' at Worstead, living in 'the utmost harmony and affection'. But Emma was far from happy. Not wishing to stagnate at home she accompanied her husband when he was called away with his regiment. This not only broadened her horizons but presented an opportunity which ultimately proved fatal to their marriage.

George's suspicions were first raised while his regiment was stationed at Colchester, where, for comfort and convenience, he had rented a nearby estate. Reminiscent of a scene from a Jane Austen novel, one evening when they were dining at the Colchester military garrison, Emma suddenly disappeared from the mess. When a search was made she was found in the quarters of Captain Marsham Elwin, a member of George's regiment. Evidence would later be produced leaving no doubt that the two had been 'criminally acquainted' for some time before this.

Captain Elwin was by all accounts a very handsome young man with dark brown eyes, probably a throwback to his descent from Pocahontas, the daughter of an American Indian chief who had married Elwin's ancestor John Rolfe. George, after a 'disagreeable quarrel' and temporary reconciliation with his wife over the matter, rather naively felt her removal from the immediate scene of dissipation and misconduct would 'tranquilize her mind'. He arranged for her to visit her sister in Yorkshire.

Unfortunately for George, both Emma and Captain Elwin also thought this a good idea, and clandestinely arranged to rendezvous at each of the four overnight stops on the journey, repeating the same during their return. The House of Lords would later hear evidence from a waiter at a Newark inn that he had walked in on them in their private sitting room and discovered Emma in a state of partial undress. 'Her petticoats were above her knees ... I had every reason to suspect she was doing something improper'.[28]

Up until this time George's friends and acquaintances had been under the impression that he and Emma enjoyed a 'perfect state of matrimonial felicity'. Two of his neighbours at Worstead testified to the couple's apparent great affection for each other; they had often observed George's kindly indulgence of his wife. But it was an illusion as far as Emma was concerned. She was either unwilling or unable to devote herself to a man she later admitted to never having loved.

Unfortunately for George he had befriended Captain Elwin, trusted him, and the three of them frequently dined together and shared outings. During their many attendances at the Assembly Room, the hub of fashionable Georgian society at Bath, Elwin's dance partner was always Emma. This was also the world of Jane Austen who lived at Bath at the time. A keen observer of such things, perhaps Miss Austen had noticed what George had not.

George's servant, Joseph Goater, testified that in the morning after regimental parade Elwin often visited Lady Brograve at Worstead House while George was conveniently not at home. At other times if unable to make a personal visit he would send her letters concealed inside a book. The poor cuckolded husband was oblivious to what was going on right under his nose. On another occasion George had invited Elwin to join them for a picnic at Worstead. According to a contemporary engraving of the scene George is depicted concentrating on the view of the passing ships through his telescope. Just below him and slightly out of his line of vision, Emma and Elwin are reclining in a marquee, canoodling on the grassy bank. This image would later be printed along with all the salacious details.

Above: **Lady Brograve and Captain Elwin canoodle while Sir George Brograve looks out to sea**

As the trial progressed George came under fire from Elwin's defence counsel for allowing Emma to make the journey to Yorkshire with only a single maid-servant, rather than the 'domestic suite which was consistent with her state as a woman of fashion and consequence'. This would supposedly have protected her virtue and honour, and therefore he should accept the blame for his wife's infidelity. Several servants said they had occasionally witnessed Emma and Elwin in compromising situations, and it was obvious to them that Elwin had not been alone in his bed while staying overnight at Worstead House.

Emma made a second journey from Worstead to Yorkshire in 1806 - three years after the original incident at Colchester. George was still unaware of what had transpired between Elwin and his wife during the first trip, but he suspected that removing her from Elwin's orbit hadn't been as effective as he had thought. Determined not to be made a fool of again, he dispatched his trusty servant-spy Goater to intercept them. After questioning Emma's maid, Goater confirmed George's fears in every detail. This was the proverbial nail in the coffin for George. It became clear that Emma's position at Worstead was untenable and she could not continue to live with him as his wife. Nor did he want her to. He ordered her to pack up her things and remove herself from his house.

As the trial continued it became apparent that Captain Elwin was a young man not so much dastardly as smitten, and although he was the defendant charged with seducing and debauching Lady Brograve, it was conceded by both sides that Emma was the instigator of the affair. Three incriminating letters expressing Elwin's undying love were read to the jury. Unfortunately for Elwin, he had addressed them to Worstead House at a time when Emma, his 'darling suffering angel' was absent in Yorkshire. George intercepted them after recognising Captain Elwin's handwriting.

Every detail of Elwin's attempted cover-up was there, together with his assurances to Emma of its success. He professed he could not live an hour without her. They also contained advice as to the best means of establishing Emma's innocence, thus allowing him - in a decent gentlemanly fashion - to take the entire blame. George would not have been particularly pleased to read that they were hopeful he would soon be dead, allowing them to be together forever.

Addressing the jury, Attorney General Sir Vicary Gibbs said that no amount of damages could restore Sir George's peace of mind, and they should take care to guard public morals by not allowing the adulterer to escape with impunity. Elwin's letters eloquently pronounced his guilt and the jury had no need to retire to consider the verdict. George returned to Worstead in July 1807 with a consolation prize of two thousand pounds in damages. In February the following year the details of the trial and the intercepted letters were published and advertised for sale to the general public for one shilling per copy.

Despite having won the 'Crim Con' case, George and Emma were still legally married. But he was not about to forgive his unfaithful wife who had been so hopeful of his early death. By this time they had been separated for a year; as far as George was concerned there was no chance of reconciliation. But surprisingly - and perhaps in an attempt to save face, Emma refused to be cast out without a fight. It was a matter of principle. She sought restitution of her conjugal rights in the Court of Arches. As Sir Vicary Gibbs had pointed out, regardless of the damages awarded, George could now no longer trust his wife. He applied to Parliament for dissolution of their marriage, once and for all.

The Court at Doctors' Commons granted him a divorce in November 1808 on the grounds of adultery, and a Divorce Bill was presented to Parliament for consideration when it resumed sessions in the New Year. The interrogation of the Brograves' servants began afresh in the Lords, and by the third reading of the Bill in March, Lord Auckland moved for its postponement yet again. He wished to examine more closely the clauses regarding the settlements on the marriage, which seemed unusual. Emma's lawyer was arguing for a clause in the Bill to annul the marriage settlement, and the Duke of Norfolk suggested the insertion of a clause making some provision for her. The Lord Chancellor vehemently disagreed, citing the direct contradiction to the uniform practice of the House for the previous ten years.

Lord Auckland went one further, saying the inclusion of such a clause would be 'productive of evil consequences'. Indeed he was very outspoken on the matter. Divorce Bills were increasing in frequency and were to him a subject of much pain and indignation. He considered them to be an evil of the first magnitude which affected the character of the higher ranks of society and contaminated the morals of every class in the United Kingdom.

The intervention of Parliament was called for, 'loudly and imperiously', and he suggested the best remedy would be to make adultery an indictable crime to be punished by fine and imprisonment, and to prohibit the intermarriage of the offending parties. The prison system was already overflowing and Lord Auckland's recommendations were never adopted - no doubt much to the relief of the 'offending parties' at the centre of the furore - and adulterers all over Britain.

At last, Sir George Brograve's Divorce Bill was passed by an Act of Parliament on 28 April 1809. Three days later Lady Brograve and Captain Elwin were married in London at St. Martin in the Fields, Westminster. The happy couple settled at Elwin's country seat, Thurning Hall, part of the inheritance from his late father Peter Elwin, to which the young Marsham Elwin had succeeded about ten years earlier.

Much matured from the love-struck nineteen-year-old who stole the young unhappily-married lady's heart, Elwin gained a reputation as a good speaker with shrewd common-sense and great fearlessness. Later described as a benevolent squire and a diligent country gentleman, he and the former Lady Brograve eventually had nine children together. After twenty-two years of marriage, Marsham Elwin died in 1831 from Bright's disease, aged 47. His widow took her daughters to Paris to complete their education after their father's death. She survived almost another forty years, dying in 1870 aged 88.

Both Emma and Elwin were said to have abilities above the average, and the fourth of their offspring, Whitwell Elwin, became a clergyman who was also a distinguished scholar, writer, critic and editor of the *Quarterly Review*. This placed him in the orbit of such people as Charles Dickens and Sir Walter Scott. One of his most intimate friends was William Makepeace Thackeray, who fondly called him 'Dr Primrose'. Before publishing Charles Darwin's revolutionary *On the Origin of Species*, John Murray sought the opinion of his trusted literary adviser, Whitwell Elwin, who advised against publishing the work and suggested that Darwin write a book about pigeons instead.

By contrast, things could not have turned out more differently for the now divorced Sir George Brograve. A somewhat jaded thirty-nine year-old, he was nevertheless an eligible baronet of considerable fortune once again. He made many trips to London in the ensuing years, staying at various hotels, mostly in upmarket Mayfair and at the Pulteney Hotel in Piccadilly, famous for its royal visitors and flush toilets. Whether it was the mortal wound to his heart which proved fatal to his confidence, or the reluctance for any society gentleman to allow his daughter to marry a divorced man, the result was the same: he never remarried. He had made a new will in favour of his two remaining brothers Roger and Matthew, but while in the midst of his divorce proceedings his list of eligible heirs suddenly halved.

In the autumn of 1808 twenty-five year-old Matthew was accidentally drowned in the Yare, a tidal freshwater river which runs between Norwich and the North Sea. His body was afterwards interred in the already well-populated family vault at Worstead. Five years later George also lost Roger - his last heir presumptive - in a well-publicised suicide. His death would have far-reaching consequences for the succession of the Brograve estates.

After Roger's demise, George had but one remaining sibling. His half-sister Anne lived at Bath with her husband Doctor John Rye and their son, George Augustus Rye. In 1816 he had plans to visit Bath, and his nephew George Rye - then studying at Oxford, had sent a letter to his self-described 'affectionate uncle' asking when he might visit him at Worstead.

Sir George replied that he was about to have some necessary painting done at the house and he would absent himself for a few weeks, after which 'I shall be happy to see you. I do not know whether I shall be able to find amusement for you in the country.'[29] He mentions his cousin Mrs. Offley at Bath and her mother, Sir George's maternal aunt Elizabeth Glover,[30] who had recently died, for whom he was in mourning.

He is clearly sensible of the importance of leaving a will, since he also mentions how happy he is that his late grandmother Mrs. Jane Halcott had made provision for her great-granddaughters. In that regard his own affairs were in disarray - as his sister and nephew would later discover.

George's country life was a world away from glittering and fashionable Bath, and very different from his father's at the farm in Waxham. Regardless of his relative benevolence towards the local populace, he was obliged to concern himself with the material encumbrances he had inherited. This often put him at odds with the poor inhabitants. For wealthy landowners such as George it was a balancing act at the best of times and one which resulted in social tension and frequent covert protests against the landed classes.

Despite the exhortations of titled gentlemen waving the statute book of laws and their armies of keepers who set mantraps, the country people held firm in their beliefs of entitlement. Poaching was not a crime, but a right. The notion that England was a 'green and pleasant land' was merely a romantic myth; George and his ilk had to be constantly on their guard. While he was sympathetic to the plight of the needy he is said to have kept his dogs hungry so they would repel intruders more effectively. But the dogs were kept so hungry that they reputedly once killed and ate a keeper.[31]

This story didn't deter a desperate gang of seven poachers from a nearby village one Christmas night in 1819. George happened to be home safely tucked up in his four-poster at Worstead unaware they were hiding in his plantation and shrubbery. His game-keeper and servants were alerted by the sound of five or six gunshots around midnight, and when they ran out of the house to confront the poachers, guns were immediately levelled at them. The villains attempted their escape with George's servants hot on their tails. A gun-battle ensued. Some of the shots 'flashed in the pan' and none hit their target, but one man who received a blow to the head was captured and imprisoned while the rest got away. A rather mixed victory for all concerned.

In between skirmishes George contributed to the culture of the county in his role as one of the Vice Presidents of the Norwich Music Festival, a triennial event first begun in 1824 as a vehicle to raise funds in support of the Norwich Hospital. It evolved into a rather grand affair involving hundreds of musicians and performers.

In January 1828 George subscribed to a book by Thomas Mortimer, *Die And Be Damned, Or, A Policy Of Insurance Against Fanaticism*. The 'improper or rude' title, the author apologised, was 'designed to induce some of the fine gentlemen of the age to inspect it'. This evidently included George; his name was amongst those of several other 'fine gentlemen' on the dedication page. Five months later he was dead, aged fifty-six.

He left no valid will and there were debts to be paid. Worstead House with its park and pleasure grounds were advertised for sale. Also on the list were the manors of Worstead Hemptons, Pentons, Stapletons, Thuxtons, Wythes and Haydons. There were other freehold estates in Worstead which included several 'most desirable' farms, the Swan Inn with brew house, garden and bowling green, a blacksmith's shop and several cottages. The rectorial tithes extending over the entire parish of Worstead which amounted to about 1,600 acres were also put on the market.

Much to the annoyance of George's sister at Bath, Mrs. Anne Rye, the rest of his estate - including Waxham, was destined to fall into the hands of their wealthy distant cousin and ambivalent heir-at-law, Henry John Conyers of Copt Hall (son of John Conyers and Berney's niece Julia Matthew).

Captain Roger Brograve - On a Hiding to Nothing

Exactly one month after Berney's death, seventeen-year-old Roger (b. 1780), fifth son from his father's second marriage, was appointed Cornet by purchase in the 2nd Regiment of Dragoon Guards. Three years later in 1800 he was promoted to Captain by purchase in the 12th West India Regiment. But young Roger took a cavalier attitude to the rules. Barely a year after his promotion he was accused by Quartermaster Samuel Wilton of theft. Charged with embezzlement of money, provisions and making false returns relating to the state of the troops under his command, Roger stood before a General Court Martial at the Royal Hospital, Chelsea, protesting his innocence.

There was already bad blood between himself and Wilton. Roger had instigated an earlier Court Martial against him in Bristol, charging him with disobeying orders and insolence. During the second trial he was censured by the court for having 'reposed too much confidence in his Quarter Master'. He had made the mistake of allowing Wilton to make the returns on his behalf.

The case was brought to the notice of George III who was very much surprised to find that an officer in charge of a regiment of cavalry had not only tolerated, but authorised an officer under his command to make the returns. This was a 'deviation from His Majesty's Rules and Regulations, and a direct breach of an Article of War of a most binding nature.' While the king had declined to interfere with the process of the Court Martial he insisted that in future, officers should make the returns themselves. Roger was exonerated of all charges.

After giving the army another six years of his life Roger decided he'd had enough of military rules and regulations. He resigned and embarked on a new, more exciting career: horse racing and gambling. Described as 'amiable in manners and generous in disposition', by all accounts it would appear he had not inherited his father's prickly character or regard for financial prudence.

For Roger, like many other young well-heeled gentlemen of his time, it was a case of easy come, easy go. A windfall from the will of his Uncle Thomas Brograve in 1810 of one thousand pounds, several London properties in St Andrew Holborn and Tottenham, plus the rents and profits of all Thomas's other properties during the minority of Roger's niece Anne Gregory - helped him nicely along the way. To this was added property at Shipdham from his other uncle, Capt. William Brograve, which had devolved to him after his brother Matthew drowned in 1808.

Roger gained a reputation as a celebrated gentleman bookmaker and one of the most popular young sportsmen in London, which possibly contributed to a false sense of his own fallibility. He must have felt bulletproof as he tempted fate on a regular basis, betting large sums on the turf.

The connections between duelling, gaming and suicide were already well known by the time he fatefully backed the field against Sir Charles Bunbury's horse *Smolensko* at Epsom, early in June 1813. Originally of competent if not splendid fortune - according to evidence given after his death - he lost ten thousand pounds (roughly equivalent to four hundred thousand pounds today)[32] when *Smolensko* won the Derby Stakes. It had been even betting between *Smolensko* and the field, but a few days before the race a rumour had gone around that the horse had been seen without one of its shoes and must be lame. Consequently Roger backed the field ten thousand to one thousand against *Smolensko* winning three events.[33]

Unfortunately for Roger, who must have sobered up very quickly, this turned out be a mistake of gargantuan proportions. *Smolensko* won all three races. He had already been dejected after losing money on race two at Newmarket, and was even more so after the Derby race at Epsom, the third of *Smolenko's* races that day. Following him off the course was his valet Trilleo, Roger telling him he had just lost an immense sum of money. He approached some of his creditors in an attempt to solicit more time to pay. He had two days until the day of reckoning when bets were settled at Tattersall's on the following Monday. Unable to reconcile the situation he now found himself in, he returned to his apartments in Piccadilly at Sackville Street. In the early evening he walked the few hundred yards down Vere Street to Ibbotson's Hotel, where he knew one of his creditors was likely to be.

As he entered the crowded dining room 'throwing his eyes wildly around the company', he fixed them at length on the object of his pursuit, Mr. Richard Bayzand, a man well-known in betting circles. Another of Roger's acquaintances was seated at the table and later related the short conversation between Roger and Bayzand: "Well Brograve, how do you feel yourself?" "Among the damned" Roger retorted morosely. "Nonsense" was the reassuring reply, "sit down and take a glass of wine with us: if you can let me have four hundred pounds on Monday morning before we go to Tattersall's, I will give you time."[34]

The offer of a drink and an invitation to accompany the gentlemen to the theatre were both declined. Roger owed Bayzand three thousand pounds and was not in a convivial mood, despite the offer of time to settle the rest of the debt. He returned to his apartments unable to either eat or sleep. Trilleo later told the inquest that Roger had paced his room restlessly till the early hours before waking in an agitated state at about 4 a.m. He asked Trilleo about some keys, then went to bed but did not sleep. By Sunday he was in a desperate state, he kept to his apartments and made no effort to dress, which was completely out of character. In the evening he rang for Trilleo to ask the time. When told nine-thirty, he looked at him with a 'significant stare' and said: "What! In the morning?"

After another sleepless night and with the prospect of meeting his creditors just a few hours away, he completely lost all reason. While it was not unusual for indisposed gentlemen to flee to Europe to escape their creditors, Roger chose the other final destination. He sat up in bed and placing a duelling pistol in his mouth he grasped the butt with his left hand, pulling the trigger with the forefinger of his right. And that was how he was discovered, with the ball lodged in the back of his head.

This act was later reported rather dramatically as the blowing out of his brains, but according to the coroner who viewed the body, Roger's skull was intact. Although suicide was illegal, most occurrences in the so-called elite classes were excused by a Coronial declaration of insanity, and Roger was no exception.

He reportedly had four thousand pounds with his bankers at the time of his death. The solicitor acting for his administrator later advertised for all creditors having a claim on his estate to come forward. There were many who lost large sums as a result of Roger's death, not least the owner of *Smolensko*, Sir Charles Bunbury.[35] The ripple effect this created saw at least one of Roger's punters in court being sued for non-payment of money owed, the blame laid squarely on Roger. Bunbury also used him as an excuse for short-paying *Smolenkso's* jockey, Tom Goodisson, who had won the three races for him that day. Bunbury paid him three ten pound notes, remarking that although Goodisson had done jolly well, he could not pay more because Roger, who owed him a large amount of money, had killed himself.[36]

Anne Rye, nee Brograve - The Dilemma of the 'Half-blood'

At the age of 32 Berney's eldest surviving twin daughter Anne was a little older than the average bride when she chose to marry a London surgeon at St Marylebone in January 1795, rather than at Worstead like her late sister Julian. Four years her junior, her new husband Doctor John Rye practised at Half Moon Street, Piccadilly. A native of Suffolk, he was born at Halesworth, son of Dr John Rye senior.

No doubt Berney, the persistent thorn in the side of Norfolk's smugglers, would have approved of his new son-in-law's family. John's brother, Lieutenant George Hubert Rye had distinguished himself in battle as a naval officer, and on retirement from the Navy he joined the Coastguard service.

Sometime after 1823 Lieutenant Rye surprised a group of smugglers 20 miles north of Waxham at Cromer, and when one threatened to kill him he shot him dead, a prerogative within the powers of a Chief Officer of the Preventive Waterguard Service.

Anne's new husband John was nothing like his brother. A mild-mannered gentleman, his inclination was to improve the lives of those less fortunate. Although he gave up his medical practice in London, he lived at Bath from at least 1819, devoting his life to philanthropy. Most notably he founded The Shipwrecked Mariners and Fishermen's Royal Benevolent Society, instituted in 1839 and which still exists today.

Anne and John's firstborn were fraternal twins who both died soon after birth. Eighteen months later, just a few weeks after the death of her father Sir Berney, their only surviving child George Augustus Rye was born in May 1797 at Hopton, Suffolk.

Anne was aged 65 at her death at Bath on Christmas Day in 1828, the longest lived and last survivor of Berney's children. Six months earlier, her half-brother, Sir George, had left the family with a dilemma when he died in June that year, intestate, divorced and childless. While he was possessed of a considerable amount of real estate, his personal effects were insufficient to cover his debts and funeral expenses.

In the twenty years since his divorce, Sir George had for some reason neglected to put his affairs in order. Five weeks after his death the opinion was sought of Mr. John Dodson, a civil lawyer of Doctors Commons (later Judge of the Prerogative Court), who wrote a lengthy report on the validity or otherwise of two cancelled wills written by Sir George, both before and after his ill-fated marriage.

In the first will, dated 3 June 1799 - before his marriage - he bequeathed all his real estate to his ill-fated brother and sole executor Roger Brograve. A further £2,500 went to Anne, his half-sister. This included a bond made by their father Berney in 1784 of fifteen hundred pounds, held in trust as part of her marriage settlement. To his brother Matthew Brograve he left £4,000, and to his niece Anne Gregory, £2,500.

These cash sums were believed to have been paid by the time Sir George wrote his second will, dated 2 May 1806, six years after his marriage. He expressly revoked the first will, and in the event he had no issue he again left all his real estate to his brother Roger in tail male, and in default, to Matthew. Failing that, the property was to go 'to his own right heirs forever'. To his then wife he had bequeathed £3,000 'and all jewels and paraphernalia'. His two brothers were joint executors and residuary legatees.

No sooner had Sir George executed this second will than the infidelity of Lady Brograve was confirmed by his servant Goater. Hurt and angry, he immediately went to his solicitors, Messrs Sewell & Co., of Norwich. In his own hand he wrote and executed a codicil revoking all legacies to his unfaithful spouse. When subsequent enquiries were made by Mr. Dodson, this will was found to have been cancelled with the names on the bottom of each sheet torn off.

Since both his brothers had predeceased him, his 'sister by the half-blood', Mrs. Anne Rye was acknowledged as Sir George's only next of kin, together with his 'half-blood' niece Anne Gregory, and they were deemed the only two who were entitled to share his personal estate. However, the personal estate being insufficient to cover expenses, Anne Rye renounced administration, and she must have been very unimpressed that Sir George's heir-at law, Henry John Conyers of Copped Hall[37] (her first cousin once removed) was doing his best to disrupt probate in order to avoid paying legacy duty on the real estate, to which Anne and her family felt more justly entitled.

In a case such as this the heir would normally be the next male on the father's side - the first in line being the eldest patrilineal nephew, but since there was only one 'half-blood' nephew, i.e., Anne's son George, Sir George's estates descended in the Conyers family. This old law of heirship excluding the half-blood has been described as one of the precious absurdities in the English law of real property. Henry John Conyers was already a wealthy property owner whose reputation for indifference led to his own seat of Copt Hall falling into disrepair. More interested in hunting, his ambivalence to owning property which was superfluous to his needs ultimately led to their neglect and eventual sale.

The 1836 *Gazetteer and Directory of Norfolk* describes the parish of Waxham as 'containing only a few scattered farm houses and cottages, 59 inhabitants, and about 1,700 acres of land, lying on the sea coast between Palling and Horsey. H. J. Conyers, Esq., is sole proprietor of the manor, which was formerly much more extensive, having suffered greatly from the encroachments of the ocean, which now seems securely confined by the lofty ridges of sand hills thrown up on the beach.'

Henry Conyers had no sons at his death in 1853 and the manor of Waxham (along with Copt Hall) passed through his eldest daughter Julia into possession of his son-in-law, the Hon. Anthony John Ashley-Cooper, youngest son of the 6th Earl of Shaftesbury.

The Gazetteer of 1854 confirms that Ashley-Cooper was by then owner and Lord of the manor. A similar fate awaited the Conyers' seat of Copt Hall, purchased by Julia's great-great grandfather Edward Conyers in 1739. After her husband's death in 1867 she sold it and continued to live at the Grosvenor Estate in Mayfair, where she died in 1907.

---

[28] Journals of the House of Lords, 2 Mar 1809
[29] Brograve papers, private collection
[30] Mrs Elizabeth Glover nee Halcott, sister of Sir George Brograve's mother Jane Halcott
[31] Wild Waxham, Davison C & Pestell R, , 2004, Norfolk Historic Buildings Trust
[32] National Archives Currency Converter http://www.nationalarchives.gov.uk/currency/
[33] The 2000 Guineas Stakes, Newmarket Stakes of 700 guineas, and the Derby of 1425 guineas at Epsom
[34] Anatomy of Gaming, Fraser's Magazine for Town and Country, Vol. 16
[35] Racing Life of Lord George Cavendish Bentinck, M.P., John Kent, 1892
[36] Ibid
[37] Henry John Conyers was descended from Elizabeth Brograve, Sir Berney Brograve's sister, wife of William Matthew

Chapter 9
A Diminished Legacy

The goal of landed families such as the Brograves had always been to ensure the continuation of name, seat, estate and title under the laws of primogeniture, occasionally supplemented by other devices. When she died, Mrs. Anne Rye's son George Augustus Rye was still unmarried at the age of 31, and acutely aware that not only was the name of Brograve suddenly extinct with his uncle Sir George's death, but also the baronetcy. As if that were not bad enough, while George was now his uncle's closest blood-relation, his late mother's wealthy cousin was enjoying his rightful inheritance.

The cash bequests George received from his Brograve relatives were invested on his behalf until he turned 21. His great uncle Thomas Brograve of Springfield Place left him £4,000 specifically for his maintenance, education and establishment in the world. With a further £1,100 from Thomas's sister Anne yet to come, George entered Exeter College, Oxford, in 1815, later changing to St Alban Hall. Although he spent at least fifteen years at Oxford, he took no degree.[38] Aware that the connection between his Brograve ancestors and their estates was now irrevocably lost, he hoped there was still some recourse to address the combined issues of extinction of name and baronetcy. Within a year or two of his uncle's death he became determined to pursue this.

The extinction of a family name can be attributed to the centuries-old and peculiarly English habit of a wife adopting the name of her husband, thereby wholly obliterating her own maiden name. This had proved a difficult problem for more than 300 years for the landed classes, which relied on successive heirs to maintain continuity. Added to this was the phenomenon of a demographic crisis in the late seventeenth and early eighteenth centuries, during which the proportion of males who left no sons to survive them promoted the probability of extinction in the male line, thus precipitating the practice of name changing.

Up until this time the Brograves had been fortunate to avoid a crisis of succession by producing enough male heirs in an unbroken line without having to resort to a collateral branch. For the name to continue, George Rye had but one option. He was prepared to take the rather drastic step of abandoning his patrilineal name and coat of arms in favour of those of his maternal forebears.

The more he thought about it, the more single-minded he became, and he discussed with his father what best course of action to take. John Rye had long ago removed himself from the orbit of his powerful and influential London friends, and by his own admission scarcely knew where to turn for counsel or assistance. He solicited the 'friendly advice' of his old acquaintance William Pleydell-Bouverie, 3rd Earl of Radnor. His undated letter[39] briefly outlines his son's quest, complaining that his uncle 'Sir George died intestate and by the barbarous injustice of our land in excluding the half-blood from all right of inheritance, his estates instead of descending to his sister's children as his nearest kin, passed to a very remote connection'.

Doctor Rye was at pains to point out that while George felt very strongly, he himself had no personal aspirations for his son to be honoured with a title. He thought although George 'may not possess properly enough to justify his aspiring to a baronetcy by a new creation', considering his long line of ancestry 'he might perhaps be deemed not undeserving of the favour of the Crown on a humble appeal to have the Brograve baronetcy revived in his person.'

So began a series of correspondence between George Augustus Rye, his father John, Sir George Naylor (Garter, College of Arms), and their intermediary, Edward Robert Porter, Clerk of the Warrants in the Court of Common Pleas. On perusal of the Brograve pedigree Naylor had agreed with George that he was the only person entitled to pursue such a claim, which would have better chance of success if some 'person of rank' used their influence. The only likely chance, he cautioned, although by no means certain, was to firstly apply for the change of name. In the event this was granted, the petition could then be presented for the revival of the baronetcy in the new name.

But he had his doubts. This did not bode well for George, since Naylor was the king's principal advisor on such matters. In May 1830 Naylor wrote to Porter: 'As however Mr. Rye seems to object to this arrangement, I should really advise him to relinquish the idea altogether.'

On the question of using some person of rank, George wrote to Porter: 'Of friends possessing interest with Ministers, I have hitherto not thought - but my father has several to whom he would apply if such a measure were required or likely to facilitate my purpose.' Porter warned there would be costs incurred if his suit was successful, but George brushed this off, saying he was 'quite aware' of them, implying money was no object as long as he achieved his goal. He became resolute to the point of obstinacy. George rejected Naylor's earlier advice, telling Porter he would not apply for the change of name unless the title was granted.

> 'As to name and arms, I am willing to relinquish those which I now bear if doing so would conduce to the success of my application - and as Sir George Naylor when in Bath intimated as much, you may consider this point as settled. My mind having been made up in all preliminary considerations previously to my resolve of presenting my petition, I have really nothing left to consider, and I now seek nothing but to try what success my appeal will meet. For disappointment I am prepared, being sensible that my patrimony does not equal what is generally required.' On the other hand he was very hopeful that 'the strong claim from a long line of ancestry on which I [base] my pretensions may meet so much

favour on the part of His Majesty as to induce his Ministers to abate in what they would otherwise be quite right in requiring.'

Somehow George was dissuaded from his all-or-nothing approach and he pursued firstly the name change only. In early May 1831 the Home Secretary William Lambe, 2nd Viscount Melbourne (later Prime Minister), sent a letter to the College of Arms emblazoned with the king's signature, bearing greetings to 'Our Right Trusty and Entirely Beloved Cousin and Councillor, Bernard Edward Howard, Duke of Norfolk, Earl Marshall and Hereditary Marshall of England'. The letter mentioned that George's desire for the name change was 'from motives of affectionate regard' for his honoured mother, and also his grandfather Sir Berney Brograve.

William IV had ascended the throne just eleven months earlier, after the death of his brother George IV, and he was right in the middle of a crisis on Electoral Reform when the Home Secretary thrust George's petition under his nose. There was also the small matter of his Coronation which he was hoping to dispense with. In the midst of these preoccupations His Majesty gave his Royal Seal of approval by flamboyantly scrawling 'William R' across the top of the letter to his 'entirely beloved cousin' Bernard Howard, whose necessary final approval as Earl Marshall was duly granted.

The good news was conveyed to George in early July when Porter wrote enclosing a copy of a letter from Sir George Naylor at the Earl Marshall's Office, advising of the success of the change of name application, and could he please deposit one hundred pounds into Porter's bank account as part payment of the fees. When the Royal Warrant arrived it was beautifully handwritten and embellished with the arms and motto of Brograve: *Finis dat esse* - which roughly translates as 'death gives us (real) being'. In retrospect, George might have thought something more along the lines of *dat mortem capitis* - or 'death gives our descendants a (real) headache',[40] would have been more accurate.

Now with part one of the plan accomplished, Porter expressed his hope that the second petition for the baronetcy would meet with the same success. In anticipation of which, George married 31 year-old Miss Mary Hawker, daughter of the 'very eminent scarlet dyer' John Hawker of Dudbridge, Gloucestershire. Hawker was an Honorary Member of the Geological Society of London, avid fossil collector and personal friend of Sir Joseph Banks.[41]

In order not to confuse family and friends, the marriage announcement was in the name of Brograve-Rye, but George dispensed with his patronym entirely not long afterwards. Mary, who came with a dowry of five thousand pounds, had quite probably crossed George's path initially after she moved with her widowed mother Sarah to lodgings at Bath in St James's Square, sometime after 1826.

Mary's father had left instructions for his wife in his will in case his eldest daughter married without her mother's approbation, 'circumstances which I hope will not take place'. George's credentials were impeccable and he was thus deemed a worthy son-in-law. Mary also had a rather useful connection; her uncle Joseph Hawker was then Richmond Herald at the College of Arms where he rubbed shoulders with Sir George Naylor, the conduit George needed to the king's ear.

In fact, Hawker and Naylor (at that time York Herald) marched beside each other in the funeral processions of the Duke of Kent in February 1820, then a few days later the Duke's father George III who died six days after his son; followed by George IV in 1830; William IV in July 1837, and Princess Augusta in 1840 - not to mention all the occasions in between. Hawker, whose portrait now hangs in the Great Hall of the College of Arms, died childless in 1846 leaving Mary Brograve and her sister the residue of his estate.

In George's petition for the baronetcy, addressed to the 'King's Most Excellent Majesty', he gives a quick run-down explaining that Charles II was graciously pleased to advance Sir Thomas Brograve of Hamels to the dignity of a Baronet in 1662, the Baronetcy having become extinct in 1707. 'Your Majesty's Royal Father King George III in blessed memory and consideration of the antiquity of the family of Brograve' revived the baronetcy in the person of Sir Berney Brograve in 1791. He reminds His Majesty that the only two grandchildren of Sir Berney still living are himself and his cousin Lady Anne Beauchamp Proctor (nee Gregory), and is therefore most desirous that the honour be revived in his person.

George's prose is typical of a person seeking royal favours: "Your Majesty's Petitioner therefore most humbly prays that Your Majesty will be graciously pleased to take the circumstances of his case into Your Royal Consideration and to grant unto him the dignity of a Baronet as heretofore enjoyed by his grandfather and the other Branches of his Family".[42]

He was hopeful, but not overly confident after Sir George Naylor's not-so-subtle hints regarding his chances. It was not to be. The letter that later arrived at No. 2 Johnstone Street bearing the news that there would be no Sir George Augustus Brograve, 3rd Baronet, put an end to what had been an anxious wait. Destined to remain plain Mr. and Mrs., George and Mary settled into their married life at Bath with the usual hopes and expectations of any newlywed couple.

It was a case of downsizing for Mary. She and her younger sister Elizabeth had grown up in the grandly proportioned Dudbridge House near Stroud, built by her grandfather Richard Hawker in 1770. Her new home, a narrow-fronted three-storied terrace house (plus the usual attic and cellar) at Johnstone Street, with the inescapable proximity of another similar row of terraces directly opposite, must have seemed to Mary a shoebox by comparison. Her sister on the other hand had merely exchanged one large house for another. Twelve years earlier at the age of seventeen she had married Walter Matthews Paul, heir to the Highgrove estate near Tetbury, now home to H.R.H Charles, Prince of Wales.

As far as can be determined, it appears the two families of Hawker in Essex and Gloucestershire which provided wives for both George and his grandfather Sir Berney were unrelated. George's father-in-law

John Hawker had distinguished himself in the eyes of King George III as the man to assist Sir Joseph Banks in carrying on an experiment to ascertain whether fine Merino wool could be produced in England.

The king, with the aid of Banks, founded a flock at Windsor comprising 44 Merinos from France and two ewes and two rams smuggled out of Spain. John Hawker was given the task of dying the wool. The king was suitably impressed when he and his entourage visited Hawker in 1788 to inspect his dye works at Dudbridge, where reputedly 'seven furnaces were continually employed and often forty-two pieces of cloth dyed in one day'. The experiments continued until at least 1791 when Hawker wrote to Sir Joseph Banks asking that he convey to the king his thanks for 'his Majesty's Goodness in having destined for me a spannish Ram'.[43]

As we have seen in earlier chapters, Sir Berney Brograve was often in the peripheral orbit of William Windham of Felbrigg M.P., later Secretary of War. More than twenty years after Berney's death, an indecorus association with a collateral branch of this family occurs in connection with a member of the Hawker family. In an all-too familiar tale, George Brograve's brother-in-law Richard Hawker was found guilty in 1820 of Criminal Conversation with Frances, the unhappy young wife of William Miller of Ozelworth. She was the daughter of the Hon. William Wyndham, himself the son of Charles, 2nd Earl of Egremont, and a cousin of the Secretary of War.

Richard Hawker was described as the son of an opulent dyer and a Fellow of Merton College, Oxford. He first began an affair with Mrs Frances Miller after visiting the Miller family with his stepmother and sisters Mary and Elizabeth, two years before the case came before the Sheriff's Court in London. The salacious details of Richard's overnight stays at the Miller's house in February 1820 became public knowledge after the Millers' butler, John Ford, gave damning evidence of the lady's bedroom-hopping while the unsuspecting husband's back was turned.

Richard Hawker took all the blame upon himself, declaring his behaviour resulted from an 'unguarded moment' when he forgot the duty he owed to himself and his former friend William Miller, to whom he expressed his sincerest regret. Pleading poverty in the face of a damages claim of ten thousand pounds, 'possessed of no property whatever', he was fined twelve hundred pounds. Eight years later he inherited his father's estate including Dudbridge House and the dye works.

The Last Gasp

By the early nineteenth century the high mortality rates experienced by previous generations had largely passed, and without the need for multiple offspring - preferably sons as insurance against family extinction - wealthy families were producing smaller numbers of children. George and Mary Brograve inadvertently continued the trend. Doubtless George had hopes for a son to carry on the hard-won name of Brograve. Disappointingly, he only had two daughters.

The eldest was born about eighteen months into their marriage and named Anne Mary Sarah after both grandmothers and her mother. A year later daughter number two arrived. Mary agreed with George's suggestion and she became the second Julian Elizabeth Brograve[44] in recognition of Sir Berney's firstborn.

Still, two daughters wasn't a complete disaster; both grew up and married. Perhaps George might have a grandson who would adopt the name, just as he had, and to whom he could leave his modest property portfolio which included several houses in Bath. The legacies from his uncle and aunt Thomas Brograve and his sister Anne no doubt assisted in their acquisition. In the 1820's he purchased two freehold properties in Raby Place, Bathwick, and also a 3,000 year lease on No. 5 Waterloo Buildings, Widcombe. He had another house in Twerton East.

George was sole executor to his father John Rye, who died in 1855 aged 87. Rye seemed to have surprised himself by living so long, outliving his wife Anne Brograve by 27 years. His life span had so exceeded his expectations in fact, that he found it necessary to make nine codicils to his will, as one by one his beneficiaries died off.

A certain Mr. Norton Ingersoll - already dead when a somewhat forgetful Doctor Rye made his will - was left fifty pounds, but the codicil three days later noted this bequest was made 'without remembering he was dead, therefore of course the legacy is void.' After his father's death, George took on the role of Vice President of the Shipwrecked Fishermen and Mariners Society which his father had founded, and he was also President of the Bath and Clevedon auxiliary.

When she was 21 his eldest daughter Anne had married 36 year-old Rev. John Acres, M.A., curate of the Somerset parish of Kenn from 1847 until 1875. After clearing the final costs of the restoration of his church, Rev. Acres was bankrupted, and as a result he and his wife lived much of their married life under her parents' roof in debt to her father who had loaned him money. The close proximity of the good Reverend's in-laws in the next-door bedroom was not ideal. Whether this had any effect on his marriage is purely speculative, but whatever the case he and his wife produced no offspring. They both died of influenza within eight days of each other in January 1898.

Whatever hopes George had of a successor lay with his youngest daughter Julian, and a young man she had probably known since childhood. For at least ten years George's father John Rye had lived in Bath at No. 60 Great Pulteney Street, a few doors along from Captain John Long and his family, who lived at No. 56. The Longs had moved permanently to Bath after Captain Long, in a rather unwise move, had sold his largest and most valuable assets: two inherited estates in Wiltshire - both with grand mansions, at Monkton Farleigh and East Coulston. Much of the money was later lost in failed London investments.

The Longs were well-known Wiltshire gentry. They could trace their lineage back to at least the 14th century, so George must have felt some confidence when in 1857 he gave his consent for Julian to marry the late Captain Long's eldest surviving son and heir, twenty-two year-old Stanhope Long.[45] Julian would discover too late that he was a young man with a difficult personality. In a letter to his cousin, his widowed mother Mary Long remarked that it was a hasty marriage. Hasty indeed; none of his family saw it coming. Mary was nevertheless hopeful it would settle her troublesome son. For Stanhope it was a solution to his domestic problems - namely his desire to be independent. After two unsuccessful years in the wilds of Australia he hated living back at home.

Not long from his return, Stanhope probably omitted the small detail that he had been sent away to relieve his recently bereaved and financially stressed mother of his upkeep. He was supposed to stay in Australia to make his fortune. On instructions from his father's executors, and living in severely straitened circumstances, Mrs Mary Long had for the last few years been merely keeping up appearances. She was forbidden to reveal publicly her dire situation in case it compromised the outcome of a lengthy court case to recover a substantial debt, owed to her late husband's estate.

Julian's new husband appeared to be a young man of substance and aspiration with an all-important inheritance in the pipeline. Looks could be deceiving; he had no ready money. Julian's sister Anne and the Reverend Acres generously gave up their bedroom in the Brograve household temporarily to accommodate the newly-weds. Determined not to share a roof with his in-laws any longer than necessary, Stanhope managed to squeeze a little money from his father's executors and took his new bride off to Devon where he had taken a lease on Puddington Lodge, a large and suitably impressive Italianate-style house on twenty-one acres.

They had a daughter and two sons before Julian decided after seven years of marriage that Stanhope did not meet her expectations. While well-intentioned, his own expectations of himself as the benevolent squire far exceeded his means. Most of his potential inheritance had been eroded by legal fees paid by his father's executors attempting to recover a rather large but disastrous investment from the bankrupt vicar of St. Giles, Camberwell. Prepared to work only as much as he thought necessary, Stanhope simply had no ability to rebuild his fortune.

Julian packed up her things (minus their children) and went back home to her family, who by this time had relocated to a large house at Atlantic Terrace East, Weston super Mare. While Stanhope did his best to divest himself of the lease on Puddington Lodge, his two spinster sisters, Katherine and Flora Long, temporarily took the children into their home at Cheltenham. Aged four, his eldest son died of Scarlet Fever while under their care. Flora wrote afterwards that Julian had not even visited her dying child. A shattered Stanhope took to drowning his sorrows. This was not at all what George Brograve had envisaged for his family.

A year later in August 1865 George wrote his will. He left provision in the event of Stanhope's inability to maintain and provide suitable education for his two remaining children, Alice and Ernest - George's only grandchildren. His doubts would prove well-founded. With no hope of reconciliation with his wife, Stanhope took to living an aimless gentleman's life in London. One night in 1870 he became the victim of highway robbery in Marylebone.

On that cool April evening he had set off from home with a few shillings in his pocket, already a bit tipsy and one thing only on his mind. Obliteration. This was obvious to at least one young opportunist amongst the minglers in Oxford Street, 23 year-old William Campion, who quickly befriended what must have appeared to him, an easy target. Just before 10 p.m a police Sergeant by the name of Theobold observed them walking arm-in-arm in Connaught Square, Stanhope so drunk he couldn't walk unaided, and together they staggered off down nearby Seymour Mews in Bryanston Square, just a short walk from his lodgings.

Prior to his marriage, the then teenage Stanhope - with a high sense of morality - had seen a thing or two in the rough and ready environs of convict-populated Australia. In a letter to his cousin in 1855 he had railed against the evils of mixing with low society and the degradation brought on by the demon drink. This was now a long-forgotten memory, and trapped in an emotional spiral of self-destruction Stanhope had become what he once so despised. That night in the mews the rubbery legs of his moral high horse gave way, leaving him completely legless.

A resident of the mews was also watching this little spectacle, and saw Campion fling his inebriated, and by now, insensible victim onto a dung-heap, where he began rifling through his pockets. A citizen's arrest was made and another nearby policeman quickly alerted. He pulled Stanhope up from the dung-heap, rudely awakening him in the process. Campion, who was quite sober, was found to have stolen four shillings and a bunch of keys.

The next day in court after a much needed bath and a change of clothes, Stanhope stood in the witness box miserably hung-over. Now in damage control he told the judge he may have been drunk on the previous evening and he thought the accused looked very much like a man he had met somewhere near Oxford Street.

It must have been obvious to the judge that despite his miserable morning-after condition Stanhope was a well-spoken and educated gentleman and his assailant clearly a rogue. Campion was found guilty and sentenced to six months hard labour. Unluckily for Stanhope, the readers of *The Times* - and probably the Brograves at Weston super Mare - were informed in two detailed instalments of his unintended close encounter with a pile of horse manure.

Whatever George Brograve thought of his estranged son-in-law we can only imagine, but it can't have been particularly endearing. To avoid further embarrassment to the family George may have been instrumental in persuading Stanhope to leave England permanently. This was an obvious and often-employed solution for a troublesome family member who became known colloquially as a Remittance Man, sent regular payments from England to stay in exile.

Whether Stanhope was indeed a Remittance Man, or just bitterly disillusioned with what his life in England had become, two years later a passage was booked for him on the steamer *Polynesian*. He sailed to Canada alone, landing at Quebec in October, 1872. He never again saw his wife or children, and twelve years later, aged 48, he died in obscurity at Elmvale, near the township of Barrie, Ontario.

George's own health was failing by this time, and he had to absent himself more frequently from his Mariner's Society meetings due to recurring bouts of bronchitis. As he lay on his deathbed, long ago resigned to defeat in the struggle to keep his mother's family name alive, he took his final laboured breath on the last day of March, 1874.

At the next meeting of the Society the gathered gentlemen lamented the loss of one who had 'worked most laboriously on behalf of the Institution, both by his personal influence and indefatigable exertions in raising funds from all parts of the country, and his well-known face will be missed.'[46]

---

[38] Letters and diaries, Vol. 1, John Henry Newman, Charles Stephen Dessain, Ian Turnbull Ker, Thomas Gornall
[39] c.1829 Brograve papers, ibid
[40] Google Translate, rough online translation
[41] Ichthyosaurs: A History of Fossil Sea-dragons; S. R. Howe, H. S. Torrens, T. Sharpe - 1981
[42] Brograve papers ibid
[43] The Sheep and Wool Correspondence of Sir Joseph Banks, 1781-1820
[44] The author's great-great grandmother
[45] Francis Stanhope Long (1835-1884), son of John Long of Monkton Farleigh and Mary Daniel. See Inquisition Post Mortem: An Adventurous Jaunt Through a 500 Year History of the Courtiers, Clothiers and Parliamentarians of the Long Family of Wiltshire C. Nicol. Forthcoming publication.
[46] The Shipwrecked Mariner, George Morrish 1873

Chapter 10
Waxham Hall

Waxham Hall
Photo copyright George Plunkett

Much of Berney's notoriety is associated with Waxham Hall, where on stormy nights his ghost is said to gallop through the gatehouse on his 'gret hoss' and rising up on his stirrups, shaking his fist at the floods and tempest, he roars angrily into the darkness in the direction of the raging sea.

From at least the 12th century the manor had passed through several private hands until it came to the Woodhouse family. They built Waxham Hall circa 1570 as a coastal stronghold against possible Spanish invasion. Enclosed on its northern side by a lofty stone wall twelve feet high on the seaward side with crocketed pinnacles and large gateway, the hall was constructed of stone recycled from three 13th and 14th century monasteries purchased by the Woodhouse family after Henry VIII's infamous Dissolution.

Pinnacled Gateway to Waxham Hall 1937
Photo copyright George Plunkett

While the remaining structure is imposing, it is a shadow of its former self. The hall was once quite magnificent with its walls faced with knapped flint, stone quoins, fine arches, buttresses, columns and a paved pond. Some evidence of these features was mentioned in the Norfolk *Gazetteer* of 1883.[47] By then part of the house had been demolished. During the First World War it was used by the military and left derelict. What remains today is now a farmhouse and the ancient timber gates have since been replaced with twentieth century corrugated iron.

The dilapidated St. John's church also suffered neglect over the years. In 1910 W. A. Dutt wrote that a quarter of a century earlier its roofless tower had been described as a 'huge pigeon locker', and the local saying, 'as blind, deaf and dumb as Waxham steeple' may have come about since the tower windows were bricked up and it had no bell. Some years prior to its partial restoration the church also served as a boathouse. A life-boat was suspended on hooks on a beam in the nave.

Waxham Great Barn west gable 1992
Photo copyright George Plunkett

The Great Barn, built in 1583-4[48] is celebrated as the largest surviving historic barn in Norfolk, and dwarfs St. John's church beside it. Measuring 177 feet long by 34 feet deep, the thatch-roofed barn is a massive structure of great historical and architectural importance. It was restored by the Norfolk County Council following compulsory acquisition during the early 1990s. It is now open to the public.

It would be years before the recurring problem of flooding was taken seriously on an official level, and its beleaguered eighteenth century owner Sir Berney Brograve did not live long enough to see the result. Three years after his son Sir George inherited the problem several thousand rats were washed from their hidey-holes when an uncommonly high tide overflowed the quay at Yarmouth in October 1800. A considerable breach was also made at Waxham.

Together, the intermittent gaps in the sand hills from Winterton to Happisburgh - either side of Waxham, measured nearly a mile in 1805. A loan was raised the same year by way of subscription after an engineer's report to the Commission of Sewers warned of the danger to many thousands of acres of land from inroads of the sea if the breaches were not repaired. Sir George Brograve led with two hundred pounds, with Robert Rising contributing one hundred. Rising had purchased the waterlogged Horsey estate from Sir George in 1803, which, due to the flooding problem was then of little value.

Possibly the general perception of its lowly worth partly compounded the difficulties for Berney in his attempts to garner support for reparation of the sea breaches. Some years later a surgeon from North Walsham, William Hewitt, expressed the widely-held view that 'Horsey next the Sea must have been formerly one of the most uninviting hamlets ever beheld. It lies between Waxham and Winterton, and is eleven miles north by west of Yarmouth. Its lonely situation, its containing a large lake, called Horsey-mere, and intersected with ditches of stagnant water, cannot render it even now prepossessing. And were it not for its complete exposure to wind from every quarter, it probably would be very unhealthy.'[49]

Hewitt remarked that 'such a singular aspect did it assume some years since, that an early historian, alluding to Horsey, recommended it to the notice of government, as being peculiarly adapted for prisoners of war, especially the French; observing they could be retained there readily, as there was only one road to it; and its growing roots in abundance, besides an innumerable quantity of frogs, the expense for maintaining them would be inconsiderable.'[50]

Berney would not have appreciated the irony of having enough frogs on his land to feed an army of French prisoners, and given his attitude to foreign enemies he would have felt even less inclined to accommodate such loathsome interlopers in close proximity to his own doorstep. Not to mention his indignation that his land was deemed fit for no other worthy purpose in his lifetime; the suggestion to which Hewitt alludes first appeared in 1781.[51]

After the Horsey Enclosure Act of 1812 the condition of the land at Horsey improved when the sea bank was repaired and drainage implemented, but over the years the ongoing maintenance required has continued to be a never-ending battle against the tide. In 1922 it was recorded that no serious breach had occurred for over a century due to the ongoing efforts of the Commissioners of Sewers, but sixteen years later in 1938 there was yet another devastating inundation.

In an all-too familiar scenario, a particularly ferocious storm lashed the east Norfolk coast causing havoc from high waves driven by a north-westerly gale. Such was their force that more than 1,500 feet of sand dunes were demolished at Horsey, allowing salt water to flood almost 7,500 acres of low-lying hinterland.

The sea rushed through the breach, sweeping away cattle and horses, fence posts, gates, haystacks and reeds. The powerful surge carried away a wooden bridge which was stopped only by a belt of trees. Waxham Hall and the nearby church were left seemingly adrift in a lake which spread as far as the eye could see. Roads were impassable for miles and a few days later falls of heavy snow added to the scene of desolation. The effect on the environment was overwhelming and long-lasting. Even with some of the pumps operating day and night it took several months to drain the water, revealing a desolate rust-red expanse of once green marsh which remained unproductive for years afterwards. Trees and fish were killed, and even the insects that once populated the marshland. Although the 18th century press reports were brief and lacking in detail, this must have been the sort of devastation Berney was faced with time and time again.

He placed much importance on his farm at Waxham. The illness and death of so many of his family members following the repeated flooding throughout 1791 renewed his resolve to have the sea breaches repaired, but inexplicably he did not relocate his wife and children to the alternative high and dry and probably superior residence of Worstead House, about ten miles inland to the west.

As William Hewitt had observed not much more than fifty years after the 1791 floods, it was generally recognised the catastrophe had contributed to a great many premature deaths. Few if any of these inhabitants would have had any other choice but to remain in their homes.

Just over two hundred years later in 2008 the battle continued in earnest - not only against the rising tide, but also against bureaucracy. The Save Our Broads group was formed by worried villagers to oppose the government agency Natural England's proposal to allow the six villages of Horsey, Sea Palling, Waxham, Potter Heigham, Hickling and Eccles to be surrendered to the sea. This was one of four options discussed behind closed doors as a knee-jerk reaction to predictions of rising sea-levels due to global warming. For Berney, surrender would never have been an option.

In winter, Horsey Mere is an internationally important wildfowl refuge, and home to thousands of ducks including teal, wigeon and pochard. Fortunately the government dismissed the idea and pledged one hundred million pounds to reinforce sea defences, thereby giving the several hundred inhabitants of Berney's old stamping ground a reprieve for the next fifty years, at least.

Worstead House

Over a period of five hundred years Worstead grew into a populous town renowned as a centre for woollen manufacture, giving its name to the world-famous cloth. It is now a small village but its past glory is reflected in the disproportionate grandeur of St Mary's church, featured in the contemporary village sign. The village itself consists of a main street and a market square, where a fair was held on Saturdays until 1666 when the threat of plague closed it down.

In June 1768, before his second marriage, Berney had renewed the lease for twenty-one years on the manor of Worstead which entitled him to receive the rectorial tithes. Another house once stood on the site – Muckley Hall - and it may have been Berney who demolished it with the intention of rebuilding. Also in 1768 he subscribed to a book of original architectural designs, and later employed architect James Wyatt to design Worstead House. The main body of the house, with its three bays, bowed front and cupola roof, was reminiscent of the larger Heaton Hall near Manchester, also designed by Wyatt, begun in 1772 and mostly completed in 1789. While still a rather grand affair, the narrower façade of Berney's house suggests an earlier design which predates the more elaborate Heaton.

Worstead House was built on a rise commanding a view of Worstead's beautiful church,, and Wyatt had designed one of the rooms with a Pompeian theme. According to *Burkes and Savills Guide to Country Houses* (Vol. III, 1981), *Country Life* and several other publications, Wyatt, who became one of the most prominent British architects of his generation, supposedly built the house between 1791 and 1797. This cannot be correct. In 1781 it was 'esteemed by travellers to be the neatest *box* in Norfolk'.[52]

Berney's earlier thank-you letter to Lord and Lady Townshend states it was written at Worstead in 1768, although the house is not specifically named. The diary of Mrs. Mary Hardy[53] mentions that on the last Sunday of October 1774, Berney had called on her husband William and the two men went together to Worstead House where they discussed some business over dinner.

Worstead House 1818.
Engraving by J.P Neale

Further confirmation of the earlier date is provided by the London newspaper that reported the death of his daughter Charlotte the following year: his address was 'Worstead House in the county of Norwich'.[54] It might therefore be assumed Worstead House was built sometime between 1768 and 1774 after the young Wyatt had returned from studying in Italy and was still relatively unknown.

The Worstead estate was purchased by the Hon. William Rous (brother of the Earl of Stradbroke), in whose family it remained for the next 110 years. Originally a symmetrical three-storied construction of red brick with walls of almost equal proportions on each side, it later had a large extension added by the new owner.

When sold by the Hon. W. Keith Rous in July 1938, *The Times* noted the uncommon feature of a large area called "The Islands", intersected by canals fifteen feet wide and five feet deep, crossed by several ornamental bridges and interlaced to form an aquatic maze with boathouses and an octagonal summerhouse in the centre. These canals apparently had been built long ago at some considerable cost, purely for the owner's amusement - as a sort of private rural mini-Disneyland.

In the *History and Antiquities of the County of Norfolk*, Vol. 9 (M.J. Armstrong, 1781), Worstead House is described as having been judiciously ornamented by Sir George's father Berney, with a canal and plantations etc., and while it may be that the islands were the work of Berney - the builder of drainage canals at Waxham - it seems at odds with his character to have created something purely for pleasure. More probably Sir George added to it after Berney's death.

By the twentieth century the house had become run down, and its new owner, the newspaper mogul Harold Harmsworth, Viscount Rothermere, demolished it with the intention of rebuilding. The outbreak of World War II changed his plans and it was never rebuilt.

Before it was demolished in 1939 Worstead House comprised twenty-one bedrooms, four bathrooms, a library and five reception rooms overlooking a ten acre lake on the estate, which amounted to about 1,900 acres in total. This included the 300 acre timbered park, eight farms, several smallholdings and 30 cottages.

Berney's grand stable block and coach houses still survive but are now derelict. The careful and detailed late neo-classical design is believed to have also been the work of James Wyatt. Built in a half-H plan with two storeys, the roof of the stables is crowned by a central tall cupola with clock, surmounted by an octagonal open lantern supporting the dome. This building may have been where Berney housed most of the sixty horses he had offered to Marquis Townshend to help equip an army of militia in 1795. The islands have also survived.

---

[47] William White's History, Gazetteer, and Directory of Norfolk, 1883
[48] Dendrochronology tests have shown that the trees for the timber were felled at this date
[49] Hewitt ibid
[50] Ibid
[51] History and Antiquities of the County of Norfolk (Vol. 7), 1791
[52] History and Antiquities of the County of Norfolk, Mostyn John Armstrong, 1781
[53] Mary Hardy's Diary, p127, by Mary Hardy, B. Cozens-Hardy, 1968
[54] Morning Post and Daily Advertiser (London), Tuesday, September 19, 1775; Issue 904

Chapter 11
Extinction of a Dynasty

The demise of the family had been a long time coming. In the thirteenth century the Brograves had their roots in Warwickshire in the person of Sir Roger Brograve, eventually branching out to Kent, where in 1472 a large estate at Kelseys was established by his descendant William Brograve, draper and citizen of London. The family prospered, and the extent of their wealth is implied by the amount of Hearth Tax paid in 1664 on 12 hearths by his descendant. Kelseys remained their country seat for 220 years until its sale in 1690.

During this period one of William's grandsons had established a family line in Northamptonshire. Another grandson (Sir Berney Brograve's great-great-great-great grandfather) rose to become a well-known and highly respected lawyer. This was Sir John Brograve, educated at Cambridge University and Gray's Inn, who in 1576 was described as 'very learned, poor, smally practised, [and] worthy of great practise'.

Someone agreed with this assessment and Sir John was appointed to the lucrative post of Attorney General for the Duchy of Lancaster under Queen Elizabeth and James I. His greatly improved financial position enabled him to build a new house at Hamels in the parish of Braughing, circa 1580. Sir Henry Chauncy wrote in his *Historical Antiquities of Hertfordshire* that Sir John 'bought several parcels of land of divers men which lay contiguous together and built a neat and uniform pile of brick, near a pleasant grove, with four turrets on the four corners thereof which do adorn the house, situated upon a dry hill where there is a pleasant prospect to the East'.

Sir John served as *custos rotulorum* for the county of Hertford for thirty years, and ten years before his death he was knighted by James I. His son Simeon succeeded him at Hamels in 1613 and the future looked rosy. Like his father, Simeon attended Cambridge and was 'bred up at Gray's Inn', followed by his two younger brothers Charles (d. 1602), and John (d. 1625), depicted in an elaborate monument at St. Mary's church, Braughing.

Simeon was married for 45 years to Dorothy Leventhorpe who bore him fourteen children, the eldest of which was John Brograve of Albury Lodge, one of Cromwell's commissioners for the county of Hertford. Simeon's grandson Thomas (son of John), was created a baronet in March 1662–3 and died in 1670, the same year as his father. Still the family prospered, but within a generation nearly all that had been accumulated would be lost.

Sir Thomas's six-year old son John succeeded him and inherited the estates at Hamels and elsewhere. Chauncy pays tribute to the young baronet who was 'proper in Stature, comely in Person, beautiful in Aspect, and strong in Body, endowed with great natural and acquired Parts, and a good Competency of Learning'.

After attaining his majority Sir John devoted his energies to enlarging Hamels, making the house 'graceful and pleasant to his Eye; he enlarg'd his Park, and adorn'd his House with several delicious Walks without, made his Rooms curious within', decorated with murals of famous battles in some rooms and walnut wainscots in others. He adorned the hall with weaponry 'plac'd in great and curious Order'. With his magnificent show-place completed, the young and very eligible bachelor was ready for marriage.

It was normal practice for the heir of an established family to marry an heiress with equivalent or near equivalent property to his own. There would have been no shortage of good prospects but Sir John's well-laid plans went awry in 1691, when, at the age of twenty-seven, he died in London from smallpox. Sickness and death was so commonplace that it was taken for granted, and thanks to the often lethal ministrations of doctors the lives of younger brothers could be transformed overnight.

Such was the case for one in particular, waiting expectantly in the wings. Sir John's younger brother Thomas junior - the spare heir - succeeded him as 3rd Baronet. Wasting little time, six months later the newly wealthy and status-enhanced twenty-two year-old Sir Thomas married Elizabeth, daughter of William, 2nd Baron Maynard. Had Sir Thomas's position not been suddenly elevated he may not have found himself a wife from the ranks of the nobility, but the speed with which the marriage took place suggests the Maynards had possibly already considered the heir to Hamels - whether Sir John or Sir Thomas - as a suitable son-in-law. He turned out to be a rather unworthy successor, however. Having such a fortune fall unexpectedly into his lap seems to have gone to his head, later prompting one contemporary writer to label him 'a poor silly man'.

This was quite a contrast to the reputation of his father Sir Thomas senior, a gentleman 'very dear' to the Vice Chancellor of Cambridge, Dr. John Lightfoot[55] 'on account of his delight in rabbinical learning'. Sir Thomas senior was described as noble and worthy by their mutual friend, the Oriental scholar Dr. Edmund Castell, although admittedly his praise at the time may have been influenced by the promise of a solicited subscription to one of Castell's new publications.

Poor silly Sir Thomas junior spent extravagantly and dissipated his inheritance to the point where in 1702 he petitioned Parliament to allow the sale of some of his property to pay his mounting debts. This was only a temporary respite however, and after his death in 1707 at the age of thirty-seven, the full extent of his liabilities was revealed. After the death of his sister Jemima, several properties including Hamels and Albury Lodge were sold in 1712 by order of the Court of Chancery to Ralph Freeman, one of Sir Thomas's creditors.

This is an often repeated example of how some family fortunes have been lost when an established and valuable estate passed from the secure management of the intended heir into the incompetent hands of a younger son. Since Sir Thomas had no children or younger brother, his baronetcy became extinct. The wreckage of his estate was entailed on the heirs of his cousin Edward Brograve (d.1710), Sir Berney Brograve's uncle.

Sir Berney is descended from Simeon Brograve's fourth son, an earlier Edward (d.1654), who inherited property from his father in Braughing. Edward also had fourteen children and was the progenitor of three generations of Thomas Brograves in a direct line: his son of Old Hall Green, Standon in Hertfordshire; his grandson of Great Dunham, Norfolk; and his great-grandson of Great Baddow near Chelmsford in Essex. This last Thomas, born posthumously circa 1692 at Althorne, was Sir Berney's father.

The Final Curtain

After the death of Sir Berney's grandson George Augustus Brograve in 1874, there was one last living individual in Britain who bore the name Brograve. She was an elderly distant cousin from an impoverished long-forgotten collateral branch, Miss Julianna Brograve (daughter of James Brograve, former bankrupt carpenter of Bermondsey). She had earned a living as a seamstress in London until her death, unmarried, in 1885. The ancient family was no more.

As for George's grandson and sole male heir, Ernest Walter Long, he saw no reason to try and make anything of the wreckage his father Stanhope had left him, and with his doting grandparents dead, he left his aging mother Julian (who died in 1905) in the capable hands of her long-time housekeeper Frances Randall at Weston super Mare. His only sister Alice lived out her genteel spinster life at Bath, and Ernest immigrated to New Zealand circa 1886 where he founded a dynasty of his own.

In Norfolk the name of Brograve can still be found in the bricks and mortar of Brograve Farmhouse and Brograve Mill on nearby Brograve Level, both Grade II listed. Other reminders exist in two small cul-de-sacs on former family estates in Kent and Essex. In Greater London is Brograve Gardens, Beckenham, and about forty miles further north-east lies Brograve Close in Great Baddow, Chelmsford.

So too, the enduring legend continues of the notorious but misunderstood ghost of Waxham, riding his fire-breathing steed across Brograve Level.

---

[55] Dr. Lightfoot's second wife Mary was the widow of Sir Thomas's uncle Augustine Brograve

INDEX

Acres, Rev John, 84, 85
Addington, Henry, 1st Viscount Sidmouth, 61
Aldbury, Hertfordshire, 10
Althorne, Essex, 44, 57
Anson, Lord, 49, 50
Ashley-Cooper, Hon Anthony John, 76
Auckland, Lord, 66, 67
Augusta, Princess, 81
Banks, Sir Joseph, 80, 82
Bath, Somerset, 42, 43, 61, 62, 64, 68, 69, 70, 74, 79, 80, 81, 84, 100
Bayzand, Richard, 72
Beauchamp, Sir Brograve Campbell, 59
Bensley. Lieutenant William, 53
Berney, John of Westwick, 44, 45
Berney, Julian, 6, 44, 45, 47
Berney, Richard, 45
Berney, Sir Richard of Parkhall, 6, 44
Berney, Thomas, 45
Black Shuck, 18
Blake, Thomas, 46
Blofield, Thomas, 12
Bonaparte, Napoleon, 2, 32, 61
Boscawen, Admiral Edward, 52
Branthwaite, Bridget, 44
Branthwaite, Henry, 6, 7, 8
Branthwaite, Jemima, 8
Branthwaite, William, 45
Brograve Gardens, Beckenham, 100
Brograve Level, 28, 100
Brograve Mill, 4, 28, 100

Brograve, Anne
  daughter of Sir Berney, 12, 16, 68, 70, 74, 75, 76, 77, 84
  sister of Sir Berney, 46, 47, 56, 57, 58, 77, 84
Brograve, Anne Mary Sarah, 83, 84, 85
Brograve, Augustine
  Berney's great uncle, 45
  Berney's uncle, 44
Brograve, Berney Hall, 12
Brograve, Carolyn, 16
Brograve, Charles, 97
Brograve, Charlotte, 15, 95
Brograve, Dorothy, 15, 16
Brograve, Edward
  Berney's son, 16
  Berney's uncle, 44, 99
Brograve, Elizabeth
  Berney's aunt, 44
  Berney's sister, 56
Brograve, George Augustus nee Rye, 74, 76, 77, 78, 81, 83, 86, 87, 100
Brograve, James, 100
Brograve, Jane, 15, 16
Brograve, Jemima, 16, 45
Brograve, Jemima (d.1697), 99
Brograve, John
  Berney's son, 16, 42, 61
Brograve, John (d.1625), 97
Brograve, John of Albury Lodge, 98
Brograve, Julian Elizabeth
  Berney's daughter, 12, 16, 38
  Berney's great-granddaughter, 83, 85, 100

Brograve, Julianna, 100
Brograve, Margaret, 15
Brograve, Matthew, 15, 16, 68, 71, 75
Brograve, Rebecca, 44
Brograve, Roger, 15, 16, 68, 70, 71, 72, 73, 75
Brograve, Simeon, 97, 98, 99
Brograve, Sir Charles, 3
Brograve, Sir Edmund, 3
Brograve, Sir Francis, 3
Brograve, Sir George Berney, 16, 26, 42, 43, 55, 58, 60, 61, 62, 64, 65, 67, 68, 74, 78, 91
Brograve, Sir John, 97
Brograve, Sir John, 2nd Bt. of Hamels, 98
Brograve, Sir Ralph, 3
Brograve, Sir Roger, 97
Brograve, Sir Thomas, 1st Bt. of Hamels, 3, 98, 99
Brograve, Sir Thomas, 3rd Bt. of Hamels, 10, 44, 81, 98, 99
Brograve, Susannah, 12
Brograve, Thomas
Berney's son, 16
Brograve, Thomas of Great Baddow, Essex
Berney's father, 6, 7, 8, 36, 44, 45, 49, 56, 100
Brograve, Thomas of Great Dunham, Norfolk
Berney's grandfather, 44, 99
Brograve, Thomas of Old Hall Green, Hertfordshire, 99
Brograve, Thomas of Springfield, Essex, 8, 9, 36, 38, 46, 47, 48, 55, 56, 57, 58, 71, 77, 84
Brograve, William, 97
Brograve, William of Shipdham, 47, 49, 50, 52, 53, 55, 71
Broome Place, Norfolk, 38

Bunbury, Sir Charles, 72, 73
Burke, Edmund, 36, 38
Butcher, Robert, 56
Byng, Admiral John, 50, 52
Cambridge University, 8, 97, 99
Campion, William, 86, 87
Carbold, James, 18
Carnarvon Earl of Highclere Castle, 59
Castell, Dr Edmund, 99
Catherine the Great, 39
Cawdor, Lord, 41
Charing-Cross, London, 8
Chauncy, Sir Henry, 97, 98
Chelmsford, Essex, 8, 9, 46, 61
Chesshyre, Peter, 44
Cliffen, Frances, 55, 56
Conyers, Edward of Copt Hall, 76
Conyers, Henry John of Copt Hall, 56, 58, 70, 75, 76
Conyers, John of Copt Hall, 56, 57, 58, 70
Conyers, Julia, 76
Cooke, W.H, 3
Darwin, Charles, 67
Defoe, Daniel, 28
Dickens, Charles, 67
Dodson, John, 74, 75
Drury, General Alexander, 33
Dudbridge House, Stroud, Gloucestershire, 81, 83
Duke of Kent, 81
Duke of Norfolk, 66, 79
Dutt, W.A, 90
Eccles, Norfolk, 29, 93
Edwards, George, 30
Elwin, Captain Marsham, 60, 63, 64, 65, 66, 67
Elwin, Peter, 67
Elwin, Whitwell, 67, 68
Felbrigg, Norfolk, 32

Fenn, Sir John, 31
Fishguard Bay, Wales, 41
Folliot, General, 9
Freeman, Ralph, 99
Gibbs, Sir Vicary, 66
Goater, Joseph, 64, 65, 75
Goodisson, Tom, 73
Gowen, Charles, 18
Great Baddow, Essex, 8, 9, 10, 12, 47, 56, 57, 100
Gregory, Anne, 38, 46, 48, 58, 71, 75, 81
Gregory, Mark, 38
Gregory, Thomas, 38
Gregory, William, 38
Griffenhoofe, Mr, 47
Gurney, Daniel, 23
H.M.S. Hazard, 11
Halcott, Jane, 15, 16, 43
Halcott, John, 15
Halcott, Matthew, 15
Hall, Elizabeth, 12
Hamilton, Lady, 60
Happisburgh, Norfolk, 30, 33, 91
Harbord, Catherine, 21
Harbord, Sir Harbord, 21, 31
Hardy, Mary, 95
Hardy, William, 14
Harmsworth, Harold, Viscount Rothermere, 96
Hawker, Edward, 12
Hawker, Elizabeth, 81
Hawker, Jane, 12, 13
Hawker, John, 80, 82
Hawker, Joseph, 80
Hawker, Mary, 80
Hawker, Richard, 82
Hawker, Sarah, 80
Heaton Hall, Manchester, 94
Hewitt, William, 92, 93, 102
Hickling, Norfolk, 31, 93

Highgrove House, Tetbury, Gloucestershire, 82
Hobart, Lord, 45
Hoe, near East Dereham, Norfolk, 15
Holderness, Lord, 49, 50, 52
Horsey Mere, Norfolk, 92, 94
Horsey, Norfolk, 3, 10, 12, 18, 21, 24, 29, 30, 31, 76, 91, 92, 93
Houghton Hall, Norfolk, 39, 40, 41
Hutchinson, John, 51
Hyde Park, London, 7, 8
Ilfracombe, Devon, 42
Ingersoll, Norton, 84
Jervis, Admiral Sir John, 43
Jessop, Susannah, 45
Jodrell, Henry, 43
Johnson, Dr Samuel, 34
Keppel, Admiral Augustus, 54
Keppel, Admiral George, 54
King Charles II, 81
King George II, 9, 11, 39
King George III, 38, 39, 71, 81, 82
King George IV, 79, 81
King Henry VIII, 89
King William IV, 79, 81
La Courdray, Captain, 53
Lambe, William 2nd Viscount Melbourne, 79
Lambert, Lieutenant, 52
Leach, John, 26
Leventhorpe, Dorothy, 98
Leverstone, Anna Maria, 9
Lightfoot, Dr John, 99
Lincoln's Inn, London, 8
London, 6, 8, 9, 11, 21, 34, 36, 38, 39, 41, 44, 45, 46, 47, 56, 67, 68, 71, 74, 80, 83, 86, 95, 97, 98, 100

Long, Captain John, 84
Long, Ernest Walter, 100
Long, Flora, 86
Long, Francis Stanhope, 85, 86, 87, 100
Long, Julian Elizabeth Mary Alice, 100
Long, Katherine, 86
Long, Mary nee Daniel, 85
Lowestoft, Norfolk, 28
Lyell, Sir Charles, 29
Lyon, William, 46
Marshall, William, 24, 25, 26, 29, 30, 102
Matthew, Julian Catherine, 56, 57, 58, 70
Matthew, Sir William, 56
Matthew, William, 56
Maynard, Elizabeth, 98
Maynard, William, 2nd Baron, 98
Miller, Frances, 83
Miller, William, 82, 83
Money, Colonel John, 33, 34
Montagu, Captain John, 51, 52
Mortimer, Thomas, 70
Moxon, Robert, 46
Muckley Hall, Worstead, Norfolk, 94
Murray, John, 67
Naylor, Sir George, 78, 79, 80, 81
Nelson, Admiral Horatio, 43, 60
Nelson, Frances, 43
Noakes Place, Great Baddow, Essex, 12
Norfolk Broads, 28
North Sea, 2, 29, 68
Norwich, Norfolk, 11, 16, 30, 31, 32, 33, 34, 35, 42, 43, 46, 60, 62, 68, 69, 70, 95
Old Bailey, 6, 7, 9, 36
Oxford University, 77
Paul, Walter Matthews, 82

Pearce, Dicky, 24
Petre, Elizabeth nee Berney, 45
Petre, William, 45
Pleydell-Bouverie, William, 3rd Earl of Radnor, 78
Pocahontas, 63
Pocock, Vice-Admiral Sir George, 54
Porter, Edward Robert, 78, 79, 80
Potter Heigham, Norfolk, 93
Proctor Beauchamp Admiral William, 38, 58
Proctor Beauchamp Sir Thomas William, 59
Ready, Rev. Henry, 20
Rising, Robert, 91
Rodney, Captain George Brydges, 49, 51, 53
Rolfe, John, 63
Rous, Hon W. Keith, 95
Rous, William, 95
Rye, Doctor John, 68, 70, 74, 78, 84
Rye, Doctor John senior, 74
Rye, George Hubert, 74
Rye, Walter, 3
Sea Palling, Norfolk, 3, 12, 18, 20, 21, 22, 29, 62, 93
Seven Years' War, The, 10, 54
Shipdham, Norfolk, 49, 55, 56, 71
Shipwrecked Mariners and Fishermen's Royal Benevolent Society, 74
Shirley, Lieutenant, 52
Smolensko, 72, 73
Springfield Place, Chelmsford, Essex, 38, 46, 48, 57
St. John's, Waxham, Norfolk, 12, 13, 15, 20, 90

St. Mary's, Worstead, Norfolk, 12, 13, 94
Stalham, Norfolk, 3
Swift, Jonathan, 24
Symonds, Captain Thomas, 54
Tate, Colonel William, 41
Temple, Lord, 6, 45, 46, 50, 53
Thackeray, William Makepeace, 25, 67
Theobold, Sgt, 86
Townshend, Viscount George, 10, 13, 22, 25, 32, 33, 34, 35, 40, 53, 54, 95, 96
Uvedale, Lieutenant, 52, 54
Walpole, Col. Hon Horatio, 60
Walpole, George, Lord Orford, 10, 11, 32, 34, 39, 40
Walpole, Horace, 40, 41
Waxham Great Barn, 20, 91
Waxham Hall, 1, 3, 4, 13, 17, 20, 22, 24, 29, 30, 42, 89, 93
Waxham, Norfolk, 1, 10, 12, 13, 16, 76, 91, 93
Westwick Park, Norfolk, 45
Whitwell, Edward, 62
Whitwell, Emma Louisa, 61, 62, 63, 64, 65, 66, 67, 75
William, Duke of Cumberland, 9, 33
Wilton, Samuel, 70, 71
Windham, William, Secretary of War, 10, 11, 31, 32, 33, 34, 35, 40, 61, 82, 102
Winterton, Norfolk, 11, 29, 30, 31, 91, 92
Woodhouse Family, 24, 89
Worstead House, Norfolk, 42, 62, 63, 64, 65, 68, 69, 70, 93, 94, 95, 96
Worstead, Norfolk, 2, 3, 13, 14, 15, 22, 23, 38, 39, 41, 45, 60, 63, 65, 66, 68, 94, 95

Wyatt, James, 94, 95, 96
Wyndham, William, 82
Yarmouth, Norfolk, 11, 30, 33, 39, 43, 50, 60, 91, 92

About the Author

A New Zealand-born writer with an interest in English history, Cheryl Nicol has also won writing awards for humorous short fiction. She is a direct descendant of Sir Berney Brograve.

Forthcoming Publication

Inquisition Post Mortem

An Adventurous Jaunt Through a 500 Year History of the Courtiers, Clothiers and Parliamentarians of the Long Family of Wiltshire.

Printed in Great Britain
by Amazon